C000184228

THE
NOTTINGHAM
FOREST
MISCELLANY

JOHN SHIPLEY

The
History
Press

*This book is dedicated to all supporters of Nottingham Forest,
wherever they may be, and to the memory of the great
Brian Clough.*

First published in 2011 by

The History Press
The Mill, Brimscombe Port
Stroud, Gloucestershire, GL5 2QG
www.thehistorypress.co.uk

© John Shipley, 2011

The right of John Shipley to be identified as the Author
of this work has been asserted in accordance with the
Copyrights, Designs and Patents Act 1988.

All rights reserved. No part of this book may be reprinted
or reproduced or utilised in any form or by any electronic,
mechanical or other means, now known or hereafter invented,
including photocopying and recording, or in any information
storage or retrieval system, without the permission in writing
from the Publishers.

British Library Cataloguing in Publication Data.
A catalogue record for this book is available from the British Library.

ISBN 978 0 7524 6076 5

Typesetting and origination by The History Press
Printed in the EU for The History Press.

INTRODUCTION

Nottingham Forest Football Club is unique in many ways, with achievements such as winning two consecutive European Cups, and winning the First Division title in their first season after promotion to the top tier of English football. Forest have also been associated with the introduction of historic improvements in the game of football such as shinpads, goal nets and elliptical goalposts and crossbars, as well as the use of whistles by referees. The football club embodied the true amateur Corinthian spirit that put the most honourable ideals of the founding fathers of the Forest Football Club above the pursuit of the professional line being taken by other football clubs.

This book 'does what it says on the tin'; it is a miscellany of information about Nottingham Forest – facts and statistics, stories and legend, including memories of those wonderful nights of floodlit football at the City Ground. A diarised history of all competitive games played in European competitions, the Inter-Cities Fairs Cup, the UEFA Cup, and of course, the European Cup, are all distilled into one book.

Over the years, Nottingham Forest have been graced with an abundance of wonderful footballers; however this book is not long enough to include them all. Instead, I have included a select few, recommending the many websites and other books to any reader who wishes to know more about a specific player. Also, I hope readers will not object, but I have deliberately avoided restating the full and detailed history of the Reds as there are numerous excellent histories already in existence.

Success should not always be measured solely by the number of trophies won, but in the case of Nottingham Forest – it's not a bad one. I sincerely hope that you will enjoy reading this book.

John Shipley, Summer 2011

ABANDONED GAME

One game stands out for its marvellous sportsmanship in the cut-throat world of modern football. On Tuesday evening 28 August 2007, Forest's League Cup tie against their other rival Leicester City was abandoned at half time with Forest winning 1–0, after Leicester's on-loan defender, 27-year-old Clive Clarke, suffered heart failure and collapsed during the interval. The game was eventually replayed on Tuesday 18 September 2007 and in a demonstration of heart-warming sportsmanship, the Leicester players invited Forest's goalkeeper Paul Smith to score a goal at the start of the game to reinstate Forest's lead from the first game. Leicester's gallant gesture was greeted warmly by fans of both teams, and widely praised by newspapers throughout the world. Unfortunately for Forest fans, victory went to the Foxes by 3 goals to 2. Amazingly Leicester had a different manager for the two games: Martin Allen left the club by mutual consent the day after the first game (only his fourth game in charge), while for the second game Gary Megson was City manager, having been appointed on 13 September. The sporting gesture had been arranged by Megson and Forest manager Colin Calderwood. The other notorious abandoned game was on 24 August 1968 when the main stand burnt down (see p. 67).

FOREST LEGEND –
ALEXANDER 'SANDY' HIGGINS

Born on 7 November 1863 in Kilmarnock, Sandy Higgins played for the Ayrshire club before joining Derby County in 1888. Two years later Sandy moved to Forest, where he stayed until his retirement in 1894. Sandy Higgins famously scored Forest's first-ever League goals. Forest's first game in the Football League was versus Everton at Goodison Park on

3 September 1892. The historic match finished 2–2, Higgins scoring both goals for the Reds. The Forest team for that milestone game was Brown; Earp, Scott; Hamilton, A. Smith, McCracken; McCallum, W. Smith, Higgins, Pike, McInnes. Higgins scored a hat-trick in his only Scottish International, an 8–2 victory over Ireland. He died on 17 April 1920. Sandy Higgins' son Alex, also known as Sandy, followed his father into football, playing for Kilmarnock, Newcastle United, and briefly for Nottingham Forest in the 1920s.

ANGLO-SCOTTISH CUP

Winning the Anglo-Scottish Cup in 1976/77 was Nottingham Forest's first trophy under Brian Clough's tutelage, beating Leyton Orient 5–1 on aggregate. Forest drew the away leg 1–1 on 12 December 1976 courtesy of a John Robertson penalty, and destroyed their lowly opponents 4–0 at the City Ground on 15 December 1976 with 2 goals from Colin Barrett, plus one each from Sammy Chapman and Ian Bowyer.

FOREST LEGEND – ARCHIE GEMMILL

Archie Gemmill was born in Paisley on 24 March 1947. He joined St Mirren, before moving to Preston North End and Derby County, where he became one of Clough and Taylor's key players in the title-winning Rams side of the mid-1970s. Eventually Clough got his man for Forest in September 1977, Archie making his debut for the Reds against Norwich City on 1 October 1977, and going on to make 58 League appearances for Forest, including 2 as substitute, scoring 4 goals. The dynamic skills of midfielder Archie Gemmill graced many stadiums all over the world. He won 43 Scottish caps, scoring 8 goals, his greatest accolade being when he scored that fantastic goal for Scotland against eventual runners-up Holland in the 3–2 group stage victory during the 1978 World Cup in Argentina. Cloughie left Archie out of the 1979 European Cup-winning team, obviously upsetting the wee man to the extent that Gemmill was sold to Birmingham City in August 1979. Many believe that Archie Gemmill was discarded far too soon by Cloughie. After Birmingham, Gemmill spent a little time with Jacksonville before signing for Wigan Athletic, and subsequently for a second spell at Derby County, where he again teamed up with manager Peter Taylor.

ASSOCIATE MEMBERS' CUP/ FOOTBALL LEAGUE TROPHY

Nottingham Forest have competed in this competition three times: in 2005/06, 2006/07 and 2007/08. The competition began in the 1983/84 season (replacing the short-lived Football League Group Cup), but from 1992 the competition was renamed the Football League Trophy. Since its second season the competition has attracted a sponsor, becoming better known as the Freight Rover Trophy from 1984 to 1987, Sherpa Van Trophy from 1987 to 1989, Leyland DAF Cup from 1989 to 1991, Autoglass Trophy from 1991 to 1994, Auto Windscreens Shields Trophy from 1994 to 2000, LDV Vans Trophy from 2000 to 2006 and the Johnstone's Paint Trophy from 2007 to today. Forest's record in this competition is:

2005/06	lost the Southern first round 3–2 away to Woking
2006/07	lost the Southern quarter-final on penalties at home to Bristol City after the game had ended 2–2
2007/08	lost the Southern first round 3–2 at home to Peterborough United

BILBAO TROPHY 1979/80

At the end of their 1979/80 pre-season tour, Forest took part
in a four-team tournament in Bilbao and won it. The other
competing teams were Athletic Bilbao, Dinamo Bucharest
and Botafogo of Rio de Janeiro. In their first game Forest beat
Botafogo 2–1 with goals from Birtles and Woodcock, then in
the final played Dinamo Bucharest who had beaten the host
team. Forest won 2–1 courtesy of two goals from Robertson,
one a penalty.

MANAGER – BILLY DAVIES

It's fair to say that not all Forest fans cheered the appointment
of Billy Davies to the post of manager of Nottingham Forest
in January 2009. He arrived as a Premier League failure,
steering rivals Derby County to an embarrassing relegation.
As a player he made a total of 331 appearances, scoring 26
goals, mostly for clubs north of the border, including Rangers,
St Mirren, Dunfermline and Motherwell. He also made 18
appearances for IF Elfsborg in Sweden, and 6 for Derby
County. In 1998, after hanging up his boots at Motherwell,
he was appointed manager, staying until 2001 when he joined
Preston North End as assistant to manager Craig Brown.
Brown left in 2004 and Billy Davies was appointed caretaker
manager before becoming manager, twice guiding Preston
to the Championship play-offs – in 2004/05, and again
in 2005/06. In June 2006 Davies was appointed manager
of Derby County, steering them into third place in the
Championship in his first season with the club, and on to the
Premier League, beating West Bromwich Albion in the play-off
final. He signed a one-year extension to his contract, but after
a dismal start in 2006/07, which saw the Rams accumulate
only 6 points from 14 games, Davies left by mutual consent
in November 2007. He had spent a reported £15 million

on new players, but claimed not to have had the backing of the Derby board. Nottingham Forest named Billy Davies as their new manager shortly after Christmas 2008, taking over from caretaker John Pemberton on 1 January 2009. Over the summer of 2009 Davies spent a reported sum of around £4 million to strengthen his squad, which in September 2009 embarked on a fantastic 18-game unbeaten run, including 10 victories – 5 of these in consecutive matches – ending the season in third spot in the Championship. Sadly, Billy's Midas touch didn't make an appearance in the play-offs and Forest were beaten by sixth-placed Blackpool – not really fair, but them's the rules! Unfortunately Forest's 2010/11 season ended in disappointment. Once again reaching the play-offs, courtesy this time of a sixth-place finish, they eventually lost to Swansea City 3–0 over the two legs.

On Sunday 12 June 2011 Forest announced the termination of Billy Davies' contract with immediate effect. One day later the club announced the appointment of 50-year-old Steve McLaren as their new manager on a three-year contract.

FOREST LEGEND – BILLY WALKER

A giant in the history of Nottingham Forest, Black Country lad William Henry 'Billy' Walker managed Nottingham Forest between 1939 and 1960, steering Forest to two promotions in his 21-year reign; the first as champions of the old Third Division South in 1950/51, and then from the old Second Division to the top flight, as runners-up in 1956/57. Billy Walker was born in Wednesbury on 29 October 1897, signing professional forms with Aston Villa in 1915, staying until 1933. He had 18 great years at Villa, many as captain, in which time they won the FA Cup in 1920, were runners-up in 1924, runners-up in the old First Division in 1930/31 and then again in 1932/33. In the process he won 18 caps for England, scoring 9 goals. His first cap came on

23 October 1920 when England beat Ireland 2–0 at Roker Park, Sunderland – Billy scoring on his England debut. His last cap was earned 12 years later when England beat Austria 4–3 at Stamford Bridge, although Billy hadn't played for England since February 1927. He did, however, captain England on three occasions.

Walker cut his managerial teeth with Sheffield Wednesday, guiding them to FA Cup final success in 1935. The highlight of Billy Walker's reign at Nottingham Forest was winning the 1959 FA Cup, his ten-man team beating Luton Town 3–1 after goalscoring winger Roy Dwight had broken his leg – no substitutes in those days. Despite Forest being relegated to the Third Division South at the end of the 1948/49 season, to their credit the committee decided to retain Walker's services. They must have been glad they did considering the success that was to come. One good reason for that success was the goalscoring feats of legendary centre-forward Wally Ardron. At the end of the 1959/60 season, with Forest finishing third from bottom of the old First Division, and only a year after his FA Cup triumph, Billy Walker made the decision to end his managerial career, accepting a place on the Nottingham Forest club committee. In 1963 Billy Walker suffered a stroke, and sadly his health deteriorated such that he passed away in Sheffield on 28 November 1964 at the relatively young age of 67, four short years after resigning as manager of Nottingham Forest.

FOREST LEGEND – BOB MCKINLAY

A stalwart of many Forest teams, Bob McKinlay made a club record 611 league appearances for the Reds – plus 3 as substitute, 53 FA Cup appearances, 11 in the League Cup and 7 in other competitions, making a grand total of 682 + 3. One-club man McKinlay was born on 10 October 1932 in Lochgelly, Fife. A nephew of Billy McKinlay (who played right-half for Forest between the wars), the centre-half made his first-team debut in 1954 and never looked back, helping Forest win promotion from the Second Division in 1956/57 and FA Cup glory in 1959.

FOOTBALL LEGEND – BRIAN CLOUGH

'He walks on water,' a claim made about only a handful of people since those early days of Christianity in Galilee; Brian Howard Clough was one of those few! This great, goalscoring centre-forward, whose playing career was sadly cut short through injury in 1964, moved into football management at Hartlepool United, staying until 1967 when he took over the reins of struggling Second Division outfit Derby County. By the end of the following season, Derby fans were celebrating the Rams' Division Two championship win. Then, in 1971/72 Derby were crowned champions of the First Division, Leeds having been denied the 'double' that season, courtesy of a last-game defeat at the hands of Wolverhampton Wanderers amid allegations of attempted match-fixing. Never short of an opinion, Clough outraged the FA after criticising them for not taking the severest action possible against Leeds United over their poor disciplinary record, and then upset some of his own players at Derby, calling them cheats and claiming they hadn't given their all in a game because they had one eye on the forthcoming England World Cup qualifying game against Poland. Derby chairman Sam Longson told his manager to shut up. Clough and his assistant Peter Taylor resigned, reputedly hoping that the Derby board would back down; they didn't – instead they appointed Dave Mackay as manager.

Next port of call for Clough and Taylor was Third Division Brighton and Hove Albion, although Cloughie left to join Leeds in July 1974 after only 8 months in charge. Brighton chairman Mike Bamber was furious that Clough had decided to desert his club after such a short time. There were accusations and counter accusations, with writs and threats of more writs, and broken compensation agreements. The whole episode was a sad indictment on the shenanigans that went on in English football. However, compared to the great man's next appointment, the Brighton saga was tame to say the least. Brian Clough's 44 stormy days at Leeds United ended in his sacking by chairman Manny Cussins and the United board. Upon his arrival at Elland Road, where he was seen by many at the club to be the ideal man to continue the great days enjoyed under the tutelage of Don Revie, Clough ran into a set of established stars who appeared not to appreciate his appointment one little bit, a claim subsequently strongly refuted by the Leeds players. Reputedly Cloughie told the Leeds players to chuck all their medals into the bin as they had been won by cheating. He then introduced a number of unpopular disciplinary measures considered by many to be Draconian and ill-conceived, at the same time placing some of the senior players on the transfer list. A run of six defeats in the league saw United (a not at all accurate term to describe the prevailing situation at the football club – disunited would be more accurate), slip to nineteenth in the table. Obviously, the Leeds fans were not too impressed. They turned on Clough, barracking him at every opportunity.

This must have been an awful time for Brian Clough. Leeds United were a giant among English football clubs, and had he been allowed to get on with the job in his own way, there is no doubt that he would have brought Leeds the European Cup success they hungered for. Still, their loss was Forest's gain.

One of the few managers to have won the League Championship with two different football clubs, Brian Clough strode through three decades of English football – the greatest manager never to manage the England football team, despite being overwhelmingly the people's choice. And he was a man of the people, a hero of the working classes who seemed to court controversy and thrive on it.

Born in Middlesbrough on 21 March 1935, Brian Clough made his name as a centre-forward with Middlesbrough and

Sunderland, becoming famous for his phenomenal goalscoring prowess. Playing for Second Division Middlesbrough, Clough was the leading goalscorer in 1958/59. In 1959/60, on the back of his scoring feats for Boro, he was selected for the Football League side to play the Irish League in Belfast on 23 September 1959, making an indelible mark on the game by scoring all 5 goals in a 5–0 victory. Obviously everyone was impressed, particularly the England selectors. He was chosen at centre-forward for England's Home International Championship game against Wales at Ninian Park in Cardiff on 17 October 1959 – England's first game following the retirement of Billy Wright. Sadly for Clough, he failed to shine in a 1–1 draw, England's only goal being scored by Jimmy Greaves. Eleven days later, on 28 October, Clough won his second and last England cap against Sweden at Wembley. England lost 3–2, their goals coming from John Connelly and Bobby Charlton. The selectors felt that there was little mileage in the Clough and Greaves partnership, and for the next England game, poor Brian was dropped, Hibernian's future Forest favourite Joe Baker being selected in his place. Clough still went on to score 39 league goals for Middlesbrough that season. With a centre-forward as prolific as him, Boro really should have won promotion to the top flight. The team's problems stemmed from their inability to plug the holes in their leaky defence and the best they achieved was two fifth place finishes in Cloughie's last two seasons with them.

At the start of the 1961/62 season, Clough moved to Sunderland for a reported fee of £42,000. Again, and somewhat surprisingly, they were a Second Division outfit. He had scored 197 goals in 213 league games for Boro; 204 goals in 222 games in all competitions. In his first season at Roker Park Clough hit 29 goals in 34 league games for the Black Cats, missing out on promotion to Division One by one point. In all competitions that season, he netted 34 times in 43 games.

Brian Clough was a goalscoring sensation, of that there was no doubt. In 274 league appearances, he scored 251 goals, almost a goal a game, before being cruelly cut down with a serious knee injury on Boxing Day 1962 in Sunderland's 3–2 defeat by Bury at Roker Park. After missing the entire 1963/64 season, at the end of which Sunderland won promotion to Division One, he was ready to make his comeback at the start of the following campaign. Unfortunately, Clough only managed 3 games and 1 goal before being forced to retire from the playing side of the game at the age of 29. And yes, we know it was a different game in his playing days, slower and more thoughtful, but you still had to put the ball in the back of the net, with some of the world's best and hardest trying to stop you. Clough's overall playing record in all competitions is 267 goals in 296 appearances – an average of one goal every 1.1 games!

After one disappointing season following a glittering managerial career between 1965 and 1993, Brian Clough retired from football on 26 April 1993. Two League Championships, two European Cups, four League Cups and countless other trophies was not a bad haul. Unpredictable, confident to the extreme, focussed, concentrated and passionate, he was undoubtedly one of the finest strikers and managers the game of football has ever known; a truly great man.

Brian Clough's full managerial record in 18 years at Nottingham Forest:
European Cup winners, 1978/79 & 1979/80
Competed in the European Cup, 1980/81
Division One champions, 1977/78
Division One runners-up, 1978/79
Third place, 1983/84, 1987/88 & 1988/89
Fifth place, 1979/80 & 1982/83
Seventh place, 1980/81
Eighth place, 1985/86, 1986/87, 1990/91 & 1991/92
Ninth place, 1984/85 & 1989/90
Twelfth place, 1981/82
Twenty-second place, 1992/93

League Cup winners, 1978, 1979, 1989 & 1990
League Cup runners-up, 1980 & 1992
FA Cup runners-up, 1991
FA Charity Shield winners, 1978
European Super Cup winners, 1979/80
European Super Cup runners-up, 1980/81
World Club Championship runners-up, 1981
Anglo-Scottish Cup winners, 1976/77
Simod Cup winners, 1989
Zenith Data Systems Cup winners, 1992
Competed in the UEFA Cup, 1983/84 & 1984/85

For five seasons of Clough's reign at Forest, 1985 to 1990, English clubs were banned from competing in European competitions following the Heysel Stadium disaster. Forest would have qualified for the UEFA Cup in two of those seasons. Brian Clough OBE, MA, sadly passed away on 20 September 2004.

CLOUGHISMS

'I've missed him. He used to make me laugh. He was the best diffuser of a situation I have ever known. I hope he's alright.'
Cloughie's comment about Peter Taylor

'On occasions I have been big-headed. I think most people are when they get in the limelight. I call myself Big Head just to remind myself not to be one.'
Cloughie's explanation for his nickname

'Don't send me flowers when I'm dead. If you like me, send them while I'm alive.'
Cloughie's wishes following the operation that saved his life

'Barbara's supervising the move. She's having more extensions built than Heathrow Airport.'

Cloughie on moving home

'Walk on water? I know most people out there will be saying that instead of walking on it, I should have taken more of it with my drinks. They are absolutely right.'

'I'm dealing with my drinking problem and I have a reputation for getting things done.'

Cloughie's reflections on his drinking problem

'I've decided to pick my moment to retire very carefully – in about 200 years time.'

Cloughie's comment on retirement

'I wouldn't say I was the best manager in the business. But I was in the top one.'

Cloughie on his ability as a football manager

'We talk about it for 20 minutes and then we decide I was right.'

Cloughie on doing things his way

BRIAN CLOUGH TROPHY

Early in 2007, representatives of the Brian Clough Memorial Fund, Nottingham Forest and Derby County, together with Brian's widow Barbara and his son Nigel, came together to create an official tournament between the two East Midlands clubs that Brian Clough managed. Rather than introduce a new separate fixture, the trophy is competed for whenever the two clubs happen to play each other competitively, commencing in 2007/08. Having stated that, the first game was a specially arranged pre-season friendly on Tuesday 31 July 2007,

Derby winning 2–0 at Pride Park, with all proceeds going to charity. The trophy is awarded to whichever team wins any league, cup or friendly game between the two clubs, played under the rules of that competition. In the event of a draw, the holders retain the trophy. At the time of writing Nottingham Forest are the holders, courtesy of a 1–0 victory over the Rams on 22 January 2011 at Pride Park in the Football League Championship, Forest also having emphatically triumphed 5–2 at the City Ground on 29 December 2010. The trophy, a silver loving cup with a lid, is more than 100 years old, but had never been used prior to being named the Brian Clough Trophy.

CITY GROUND FACTS

The first official Football League match at the City Ground was staged on 3 September 1898, against Blackburn Rovers. The crowd is reputed to have been 15,000. Sadly, Forest lost 1–0. Three draws at home followed, but on 15 October 1898, Forest won their first League game at the City Ground, beating Stoke City 2–1.

The record gate was somewhat larger than that first game, being recorded at 49,946 on 28 October 1967, for a First Division match against Manchester United.

The City Ground staged its first floodlit game on Monday 11 September 1961 when Forest played a League Cup tie against Gillingham. The attendance was 11,336. This game was played on a Monday night because Forest were due to play their first round, first leg Inter-Cities Fairs Cup game against Valencia in Spain two days later on Wednesday 13 September, which Forest went on to lose 2–0. They lost the second leg 5–1 at the City Ground on Wednesday 4 October and were knocked out of the competition.

A number of international games have been staged at the City Ground. The first was on 15 March 1909 when England played Wales in the Home International Championship. The attendance was 11,500 and England won 2–0. The second, a Wartime International on 18 April 1941, saw England beat Wales 4–1 in front of 13,016 spectators. Additionally the City Ground hosted three First Round, Group D matches in the 1996 European Championships:

11 June 1996: Turkey 0–1 Croatia, attendance 22,406
14 June 1996: Portugal 1–0 Turkey, attendance 22,670
19 June 1996: Croatia 0–3 Portugal, attendance 20,484
The other Group D games were staged at Hillsborough.

The City Ground has also been the venue for the following FA Cup semi-finals:

1901   Sheffield United v Aston Villa. The game finished 2–2 and was replayed at the Baseball Ground, United winning 3–0.

1902   Sheffield United v Derby County. This was the second replay, United winning 1–0 after the first tie at the Hawthorns had ended 2–2, and the replay at Molineux had finished 1–1. In the other semi-final Forest lost to Southampton.

1905   Aston Villa v Everton. Villa won the replay 2–1 at the City Ground, having drawn the first game 1–1 at Stoke's Victoria Ground.

1961   Leicester City v Sheffield United. The first game at Elland Road, Leeds, ended 0–0. The replay at the City Ground ended in the same score. The Foxes then won the second replay 2–0 at St Andrews.

1965   Leeds United v Manchester United. It was 0–0 at Hillsborough in the first game, with Leeds winning the replay 1–0 at the City Ground.

The City Ground has also hosted two Women's FA Cup finals. In 2007, Arsenal beat Charlton Athletic 4–1, with an attendance of 24,529. Then, in 2008, Arsenal beat Leeds United 4–1 in front of 24,582.

The ground has also hosted a semi-final of Rugby's Heineken Cup – on 28 April 2002, which saw Leicester Tigers beat Llanelli Scarlets 13–12 – and an REM concert in July 2005.

CHAMPIONSHIPS

In the 1891/92 season Nottingham Forest won their first championship: the Football Alliance, a league formed to rival the Football League. The final league table placings are not certain, but as Forest were champions that is not so important. It's likely that The Wednesday and Newton Heath finished second and third to Forest as these three were elected to the Football League for the following season as the three strongest teams in the Football Alliance.

Nottingham Forest have been crowned champions of one or other of the Football Leagues on four separate occasions. The first two times was as champions of the old Second Division in 1906/07, and again in 1921/22. In both cases 2 points were awarded for a win, 1 for a draw.

1906/07 final top six league placings Division Two:

	Pld	W	D	L	F	A	Pts
Nottingham Forest	38	28	4	6	74	36	60
Chelsea	38	26	5	7	80	34	57
Leicester Fosse	38	20	8	10	62	39	48
West Bromwich Albion	38	21	5	12	83	45	47
Bradford City	38	21	5	12	70	53	47
Wolverhampton Wanderers	38	17	7	14	66	53	41

1921/22 final top six league placings Division Two:

	Pld	W	D	L	F	A	Pts
Nottingham Forest	42	22	12	8	51	30	56
Stoke City	42	18	16	8	60	44	52
Barnsley	42	22	8	12	67	52	52
West Ham United	42	20	8	14	52	39	48
Hull City	42	19	10	13	51	41	48
South Shields	42	17	12	13	43	38	46

The next time Forest were crowned champions was of the old Third Division South in 1950/51. Again 2 points were awarded for a win.

1950/51 final top six league placings Division Three South:

	Pld	W	D	L	F	A	Pts
Nottingham Forest	46	30	10	6	110	40	70
Norwich City	46	25	14	7	82	45	64
Reading	46	21	15	10	88	53	57
Plymouth Argyle	46	24	9	13	85	55	57
Millwall	46	23	10	13	80	57	56
Bristol Rovers	46	20	15	11	64	42	55

Then came the best; champions of the old First Division (now the Premier League) in 1977/78. Again 2 points were awarded for a win back then.

1977/78 final top six league placings Division One:

	Pld	W	D	L	F	A	Pts
Nottingham Forest	42	25	14	3	69	24	64
Liverpool	42	24	9	9	65	34	57
Everton	42	22	11	9	76	45	55
Manchester City	42	20	12	10	74	51	52
Arsenal	42	21	10	11	60	37	52
West Bromwich Albion	42	18	14	10	62	53	50

CHAIRMEN OF NOTTINGHAM FOREST

1865–66	J.S. Scrimshaw	1960–63	J.H. Willmer
1866–68	W.R. Lymberry	1964–66	G.F. Sisson
1868–74	J.S. Milford	1966–71	A. Wood
1874–79	A. Banks	1971–73	H. Levy
1879–84	S.W. Widdowson	1973–76	J.H. Willmer
1884–86	W. Brown	1976–78	B.J. Appleby, QC
1886–94	T.G. Howitt	1978–79	S.M. Dryden, JP
1894–95	G. Seldon	1980–86	G.E. MacPherson, JP
1895–97	J. Cutts	1986–93	M. Rowarth
1897–1920	W.T. Hancock	1993–97	F. Reacher
1920–48	H.R. Cobbin	1997–98	I.I. Korn
1948–55	J.H. Brentnall	1998–2000	P.W. Soar
1955–57	G.S. Oscroft	2000–02	E.M. Barnes
1957–60	H.W. Alcock	2002–	N.E. Doughty

FOREST LEGEND – DAVE NEEDHAM

Born in Leicester on 21 May 1949, Dave Needham was a highly rated member of Jimmy Sirrell's barnstorming Notts County side of the early 1970s, making 429 league appearances for the Magpies and scoring 32 goals before being transferred to Queens Park Rangers, where he made only 18 appearances, scoring 3 goals. When Larry Lloyd was injured almost half-way through the 1977/78 season, Clough dipped swiftly into the transfer market to pick up this gem of a footballer. Dave went on to make 81 league appearances for Forest, plus 5 as substitute, weighing in with 9 goals. He missed out on both European Champions Cup finals, and sadly is often remembered for his collision with Peter Shilton during the 1980 League Cup final that allowed Andy Gray to win the trophy for Wolves. In May 1982, Dave was released by Forest, and took up a new challenge in Canada with Toronto Blizzards.

CHAMPIONS 1977/78

Summary of Forest's fixtures and results 1977/78, Football
League Division One:

Match	Date	Opponents	H/A	Score
1	20/08/77	Everton	A	3–1
2	23/08/77	Bristol City	H	1–0
3	27/08/77	Derby County	H	3–0
4	03/09/77	Arsenal	A	0–3
5	10/09/77	Wolves	A	3–2
6	17/09/77	Aston Villa	H	2–0
7	24/09/77	Leicester City	A	3–0
8	01/10/77	Norwich City	H	1–1
9	04/10/77	Ipswich Town	H	4–0
10	08/10/77	West Ham United	A	0–0
11	15/10/77	Manchester City	H	2–1
12	22/10/77	Queens Park Rangers	A	2–0
13	29/10/77	Middlesbrough	H	4–0
14	05/11/77	Chelsea	A	0–1
15	12/11/77	Manchester United	H	2–1
16	19/11/77	Leeds United	A	0–1
17	26/11/77	West Bromwich Albion	H	0–0
18	03/12/77	Birmingham City	A	2–0
19	10/12/77	Coventry City	H	2–1
20	17/12/77	Manchester United	A	4–0
21	26/12/77	Liverpool	H	1–1
22	28/12/77	Newcastle United	A	2–0
23	31/12/77	Bristol City	A	3-1
24	02/01/78	Everton	H	1–1
25	14/01/78	Derby County	A	0–0
26	21/01/78	Arsenal	H	2–0
27	04/02/78	Wolves	H	2–0
28	25/02/78	Norwich City	A	3–3
29	04/03/78	West Ham United	H	2–0
30	14/03/78	Leicester City	H	1–0

31	25/03/78	Newcastle United	H	2–0
32	29/03/78	Middlesbrough	A	2–2
33	01/04/78	Chelsea	H	3–1
34	05/04/78	Aston Villa	A	1–0
35	11/04/78	Manchester City	A	0–0
36	15/04/78	Leeds United	H	1–1
37	18/04/78	Queens Park Rangers	H	1–0
38	22/04/78	Coventry City	A	0–0
39	25/04/78	Ipswich Town	A	2–0
40	29/04/78	Birmingham City	H	0–0
41	02/05/78	West Bromwich Albion	A	2–2
42	04/05/78	Liverpool	A	0–0

Summary of League Appearances in 1977/78

42 – John Robertson

41 – Kenny Burns

40 – Peter Withe

38 – Martin O'Neill (+ 2 as sub)

37 – Peter Shilton, Viv Anderson

36 – Tony Woodcock

33 – Colin Barrett (+ 2 as sub)

32 – Archie Gemmill (+ 2 as sub)

31 – John McGovern

26 – Larry Lloyd, Ian Bowyer (+ 3 as sub)

16 – David Needham

12 – Frank Clark (+ 1 as sub)

10 – John O'Hare

5 – John Middleton

League Goalscorers in 1977/78

12 – Peter Withe, John Robertson (7 penalties)

11 – Tony Woodcock

8 – Martin O'Neill

4 – John McGovern, Ian Bowyer, Kenny Burns, David Needham

3 – Archie Gemmill, Viv Anderson

1 – Colin Barrett, Frank Clark

2 – Own goals

Of a total of 69 League goals one hat-trick was scored, by Peter Withe, who actually scored all 4 goals in the 4–0 defeat of Ipswich Town on 4 October 1977. Forest's 'oh-so-mean' defence conceded only 24 league goals.

Football League Cup 1977/78

Date	Round	Opponents	H/A	Score
30/08/77	2	West Ham United	H	5–0
25/10/77	3	Notts County	H	4–0
29/11/77	4	Aston Villa	H	4–2
17/01/78	5	Bury	A	3–0
08/02/78	SF 1st leg	Leeds United	A	3–1
22/02/78	SF 2nd leg	Leeds United	H	4–2
18/03/78	Final	Liverpool	(Wembley)	0–0 aet
22/03/78	Final (r)	Liverpool	(Old Trafford)	1–0

Summary of Appearances in the 1977/78 League Cup

8 – Viv Anderson, Ian Bowyer, Kenny Burns, Martin
    O'Neill, John Robertson, Peter Withe, Tony Woodcock
7 – John McGovern, Chris Woods
6 – Larry Lloyd
5 – Colin Barrett
4 – Frank Clark
2 – John O'Hare (+ 1 as sub)
1 – John Middleton

Goalscorers in the 1977/78 League Cup

6 – Ian Bowyer
5 – Peter Withe
4 – Tony Woodcock
3 – John Robertson (2 penalties), Martin O'Neill
1 – Viv Anderson, Larry Lloyd, John O'Hare

Forest scored a total of 24 goals in the League Cup, only 5 conceded.

FA Cup 1977/78

Date	Round	Opponents	H/A	Score
07/01/78	3	Swindon Town	H	4–1
31/01/78	4	Manchester City	H	2–1
18/02/78	5	QPR	A	1–1
27/02/78	5 (replay)	QPR	H	1–1
02/03/78	5 (2nd replay)	QPR	H	3–1
11/03/78	6	West Bromwich Albion	A	0–2

Summary of FA Cup Appearances in 1977/78

6 – Kenny Burns, David Needham, Martin O'Neill, John
   Robertson, Peter Shilton, Peter Withe, Tony Woodcock
5 – Viv Anderson
4 – Archie Gemmill, John McGovern
3 – Colin Barrett, Ian Bowyer, Frank Clark
2 – Larry Lloyd, John O'Hare (1 as sub)

The FA Cup Goalscorers in 1977/78

4 – Tony Woodcock
3 – John Robertson (1 penalty)
2 – Martin O'Neill, Peter Withe

A total of 11 FA Cup goals, 7 conceded.

Champions Forest's Postscript to 1977/78

So, that was Forest's first Division One championship-winning
season. The following season they qualified for the 1978/79
European Cup, and as we know, they triumphed, beating
Malmö 1–0 in the final with a Trevor Francis goal. They also
retained the Football League Cup, beating Southampton 3–2.
They finished the 1978/79 league programme in runners-up
spot, and won the FA Charity Shield on 12 August 1978 by
walloping cup winners Ipswich Town 5–1 at Wembley. One
year later, in 1979/80, Forest retained the European Cup
trophy when they beat Hamburg, again by the score of 1–0,
courtesy of a John Robertson goal.

CREATING FOREST'S 1977/78
CHAMPIONSHIP-WINNING TEAM

Soon after his appointment to the job of manager, Brian Clough began to assemble his team. In February 1975 he raided his previous club, Leeds, to sign John O'Hare and John McGovern, paying much less than when he had bought them from Derby; two of his old dependable players were back under his wing. John Robertson and Martin O'Neill, both discontented under the previous incumbent Allan Brown, were reinstated to the first team.

Next to join was the widely experienced full-back Frank Clark, who was secured on a free transfer from Newcastle in July 1975. Colin Barrett was signed from Manchester City in March 1976 and Cloughie's old partner Peter Taylor came on board in July of the same year. Then, in September 1976, striker Peter Withe was purchased from Birmingham City, and in October ex-England and Liverpool pivot Larry Lloyd was bought from Coventry City. In July 1977, in came hardman striker/defender Kenny Burns from Birmingham City.

They joined former apprentices, goalkeepers John Middleton and Chris Woods, full-back Viv Anderson, and striker Tony Woodcock, plus the versatile and ever-dependable Ian Bowyer, who had been signed from Leyton Orient by Dave MacKay in October 1973.

This, then, was the group of players that formed the nucleus of Clough and Taylor's team. Peter Shilton was signed from Stoke in September 1977, and in the same month, Archie Gemmill arrived from Derby County, with Leicester-born Dave Needham joining from QPR in December 1977 to add depth to the defence.

Forest's playing style under Clough was both simple and effective. A strong, well-marshalled defence epitomised their marvellous teamwork, while their passing was accurate and patient. In goal, after the first few games, Peter Shilton was outstandingly acrobatic, and in front of him, the solid and often quite scary pairing of Burns and Lloyd, plus, in the second half of the season, Dave Needham. All were reliable in the air and good on the ground, and ably supported by full-backs Anderson, Barrett and Clark. In the middle of the park, O'Neill covered the right-hand side, with the brilliant Robertson on the left supplying lots of ammunition, and in the centre, the ball-winning McGovern, Bowyer and later Gemmill providing the creativity. Up front, Withe and Woodcock chased and harried, as well as scoring goals. There is no doubt that Clough and Taylor's team included many fine individual players, but it was the way the blend worked together that made them extra-special. This is what made the Reds a Championship-winning side in 1977/78. Yes, they were fortunate where injuries were concerned, but nothing should be taken away from their achievements because of this. They were a team to be proud of. A great team spirit was forged. Everyone in the squad knew their job, as well as what to expect from their colleagues. Clough had them all playing to their strengths.

Apart from John Middleton, who played only the first 5 league games, a total of just 15 players were used in the league and FA Cup campaigns. Add one, Chris Woods, for the League Cup games, to bring the overall total number of players used in the three 1977/78 domestic competitions to 17 – surely one of the fewest ever in a Championship-winning season, which of course with Forest's success in the League Cup, was also a 'double'.

BACK TO FOREST'S LEAGUE CHAMPIONSHIPS

The next and last time to date that Nottingham Forest were crowned champions was of the new First Division (the old Second Division) in 1997/98, where 3 points were granted for a win.

1997/98 final top six league placings Division One

	Pld	W	D	L	F	A	Pts
Nottingham Forest	46	28	10	8	82	42	94
Middlesbrough	46	27	10	9	77	41	91
Sunderland	46	26	12	8	86	50	90
Charlton Athletic	46	26	10	10	80	49	88
Ipswich Town	46	23	14	9	77	43	83
Sheffield United	46	19	17	10	69	54	74

CLUB COLOURS

In 1864, the year before the formation of the Forest Football Club, charismatic Italian freedom fighter General Giuseppe Garibaldi made a triumphant visit to Great Britain, capturing the hearts and the imaginations of the British people. In 1861 Garibaldi had become famous for the major role he played in the unification of Italy, bringing together the nation states of Lombardy, Tuscany, Piedmont, etc., in the process installing King Victor Emmanuel II to the throne of a united Italy. Garibaldi's reputation as a daring and imaginative military tactician was enhanced by his many successes in battles and campaigns, aided by the speed with which the general moved his forces from one place to another. His army were known as the 'Red Shirts' because of the scarlet-red shirts they wore. It was Garibaldi's ideology that attracted the young men of the Forest Football Club to choose red as their club colour. Remember that in those days football clubs identified themselves more by their headgear than their shirts, therefore following the club's inaugural meeting, Treasurer William Brown was sent to purchase a set of scarlet-red silk caps with tassels. From then on, Forest players donned their red caps for each match. Thus Forest became the first football club to 'officially' wear red, a colour since copied by a significant number of other teams. They are the reason behind Arsenal's choice of red, having donated a full set of red kits following Arsenal's foundation in 1886, as well as providing red shirts to Liverpool.

As an aside, Garibaldi biscuits were apparently first created by General Garibaldi's cook, who devised a lightweight, high-energy foodstuff that his men could eat while on the march.

FOREST LEGEND – COLIN BARRETT

Born in Stockport on 3 August 1952, versatile defender Colin Barrett was signed by Forest in March 1976 from Manchester City for a fee reported to be £30,000, making his debut on 13 May 1976 in the game against Fulham. Barrett was equally at home in any of the defensive or midfield positions, although most pundits regarded left-back as his best role. Scorer of the fabulous goal in the European Cup tie with Liverpool that sealed a great win against the two-time Euro champions, he made 69 league appearances for Forest, including 5 as substitute, scoring 4 league goals. In June 1980, he was sold to Swindon Town.

IT'S JUST NOT CRICKET

At one time or another Trent Bridge cricket ground was the home venue for both Nottingham football clubs.

DALLAS CUP XXIII – 2002

Nottingham Forest won the Super Group U19 competition of the Dallas Cup in 2002. The Dallas Cup is the oldest international youth soccer tournament in the United States, founded in 1980 by the Texas Longhorns Soccer Club, and is held each year over the Easter period.

DURIN' THE WAR, PART I

The First World War began in the summer of 1914, but failed to interrupt the 1914/15 football season, which saw Nottingham Forest languishing third from bottom of the Second Division. With first-class competitive football ending in 1915, and many footballers signing up to fight for their country, there was a dearth of players. Most clubs fielded guest players on an ad hoc basis. The Football League and the FA Cup were suspended, and in their place four regional leagues were set up, appearances and goals not counting in players' official records. Nottingham Forest were scheduled to play in the Football League (Midland Section), but early in 1915 Forest had to advise the League that they were struggling to pay their bills. A grant of £50, plus additional support in the form of a season-long weekly payment helped Forest to survive but if it hadn't been for the war, it is possible that the club's existence might have been severely tested. Forest were winners of the Principal Tournament in 1915/16. They also won the 1915/16 Subsidiary Tournament Southern Division. In 1916/17 Forest failed to win anything, but in 1917/18 they won the Football League (Midland Section) once again. Also a championship play-off was played between Forest and Everton, winners of the Lancashire Section, which Forest won on aggregate 1–0. When the official Football League programme resumed in 1919/20, Nottingham Forest took their place in the Second Division.

DURIN' THE WAR, PART II

When British Prime Minister Neville Chamberlain got off the aeroplane waving that piece of paper claiming 'peace in our time', nobody in the country, including the Football League, could have predicted that three games into the new football season, war would be declared on 3 September 1939. Nottingham Forest hadn't begun too badly, winning two of their three Second Division games. The team was en route to Swansea to play the Swans and had got as far as Oxford when they turned round and headed back to Nottingham. The Football League abandoned all fixtures until further notice and a short time later several regional leagues were rapidly organised.

MORE CLOUGHISMS

'If a chairman sacks the manager he initially appointed, he should go as well.'

Cloughie's irritated comment about too many managers getting the sack

'I thought it was my next-door neighbour because I think she felt that if I got something like that I would have to move.'

Cloughie guessing on who nominated him for a knighthood

'I think the letters must stand for Old Big 'Ead.'

Cloughie on his OBE

'This is a terrible day . . . for Leeds United.'

Cloughie on being sacked by Leeds after 44 days as manager

'At last England have appointed a manager who speaks English better than the players.'

Cloughie's view after England appoint Sven-Goran Eriksson

'I'm sure the England selectors thought if they took me on and gave me the job, I'd want to run the show. They were shrewd because that's exactly what I would have done.'

**Cloughie's thoughts on not being appointed
England manager**

'Players lose you games, not tactics. There's so much crap talked about tactics by people who barely know how to win at dominoes.'

Cloughie's view after England's exit from Euro 2000

EAST MIDLANDS RIVALS

Forest have a 'healthy' rivalry with all the clubs of the East Midlands, but it is with Derby County that this rivalry is the most fierce. Having said that, obviously Forest's closest rivals in the professional game distance-wise are Notts County, the two grounds being a long stone's throw from each other. However, in recent times the Reds have managed to maintain a higher league status than the Magpies, despite briefly playing in the same league in 1994/95. Back to Derby County, both the Reds and the Rams have been the recipients of the magical managerial touch of the Dynamic Duo, Brian Clough and Peter Taylor, resulting in hugely successful periods. Always a lively affair, games between the two teams have the added dimension since 2007 when the Brian Clough Trophy was inaugurated.

FOREST LEGEND – ENOCH WEST

Nottinghamshire lad Enoch James West notched 100 goals in 183 appearances for the Reds between 1905 and 1910. Born in Hucknall Torkard on 31 March 1886, West bagged 4 league hat-tricks plus 1 in the FA Cup, once scoring 4 goals in one game. Subsequently he was a Division One championship winner with Manchester United for whom he also scored 100 goals.

ENGLAND INTERNATIONALS

Nottingham Forest have provided England with many fine international players. Among the most notable are:

Peter Shilton 125 caps in goal for England, 19 of them while playing for Nottingham Forest
Stuart 'Psycho' Pearce has 78 caps at left-back for England, 76 while playing for Forest – he scored 5 goals
Des Walker 59 caps, 43 while at Forest
Trevor Francis 52 caps, 12 goals
Tony Woodcock 42 caps, 16 goals
Viv Anderson 30 caps, 2 goals
Neil Webb 26 caps, 4 goals
Steve Hodge 24 caps
Nigel Clough 14 caps
Tinsley Lindley 13 caps, 14 goals
Steve Stone 9 caps, 2 goals

Of course not all caps were won while at Nottingham Forest. Among those who played for Forest but won their England caps while playing for other clubs are Chris Woods, Teddy Sheringham, Michael Dawson and Jermaine Jenas.

EUROPEAN NIGHTS

Nottingham Forest have played 50 games in Europe, winning 27, drawing 10, and losing 13. Here's a summary of the Reds' record in European competitions:

Competition	Pld	W	D	L	F	A
European Cup	20	12	4	4	32	12
UEFA Cup	20	10	5	5	18	16
Inter-Cities Fairs Cup	6	3	0	3	8	9
UEFA Super Cup	4	2	1	1	4	3
Total	50	27	10	13	62	40

Inter-Cities Fairs Cup 1961/62
VALENCIA 2–0 NOTTINGHAM FOREST
Inter-Cities Fairs Cup, round one, first leg,
Wednesday 13 September 1961
Forest: Grummitt; Wilson, Winfield; Palmer, Whitefoot,
McKinlay; Hockey, Iley, Vowden, Quigley, Gray B.

NOTTINGHAM FOREST 1–5 VALENCIA
Inter-Cities Fairs Cup, round one, second leg,
Wednesday 4 October 1961
Forest: Grummitt; Wilson, Winfield; Palmer, Whitefoot,
McKinlay; Hockey, Iley, Vowden, Quigley, Gray B.
Result: Forest lost 7–1 on aggregate

Forest were literally steamrollered out of round one by the
eventual winners of this competition. Valencia went on to
beat Barcelona 7–3 in the two-legged final in September
1962, a year after the competition started.

Inter-Cities Fairs Cup 1967/68
EINTRACHT FRANKFURT 0–1 NOTTINGHAM FOREST
Inter-Cities Fairs Cup, round one, first leg,
Wednesday 20 September 1967
Forest: Grummitt; Hindley, Newton H.; Barnwell,
Hennessey, Chapman S.; Lyall, Baxter, Wignall, Baker J.,
Storey-Moore

NOTTINGHAM FOREST 4–0 EINTRACHT FRANKFURT
Inter-Cities Fairs Cup, round one, second leg,
Tuesday 17 October 1967
Forest: Grummitt; Hindley, Newton H.; Barnwell,
Hennessey, Chapman S.; Lyall, Baxter, Wignall, Baker J.,
Storey-Moore
Result: Forest won 5–0 on aggregate

NOTTINGHAM FOREST 2–1 FC ZURICH
Inter-Cities Fairs Cup, round two, first leg,
Tuesday 31 October 1967
Forest: Grummitt; Hindley, Newton H.; Barnwell,
Hennessey, Chapman S.; Lyall, Baxter, Wignall, Baker J.,
Storey-Moore

FC ZURICH 1–0 NOTTINGHAM FOREST
Inter-Cities Fairs Cup, round two, second leg,
Tuesday 14 November 1967
Forest: Grummitt; Hindley, Newton H.; Barnwell,
Hennessey, Chapman S.; Lyall, Baxter, Wignall, Baker J.,
Storey-Moore
Result: Forest drew 2–2 on aggregate but went out of the
competition on the away goals rule

FC Zurich made it through round three at the expense of
Sporting Lisbon only to be knocked out in the quarter-finals
by Dundee, 2–0 on aggregate. In the final, Leeds United beat
Ferencváros 1–0 over two-legs.

The 1978/79 European Cup
As champions of the Football League in 1977/78, Nottingham
Forest earned the right to play in the European Cup for the
first time. During the close season, Clough and Taylor busied
themselves in the transfer market, determined to add even
more firepower to the team. In the end, all they did was
sell. After playing in the 5–0 victory over Ipswich Town in

the Charity Shield at Wembley on 12 August 1978, plus the opening league game against Tottenham, Peter Withe was sold to Newcastle United for £200,000 – some believe he was discarded too soon. However, Brian Clough felt that he had a couple of young lads on the books who were already equal to the task of replacing Withe. Apprentice Steve Elliott had played in a few friendly games in the run-up to the previous season, and now he was called upon to make his first-team debut on 22 August 1978. He played in this, and the next three league games, plus two League Cup ties; five games, in which he failed to score. Centre-forwards need to score so in came Nottingham-born Garry Birtles, bought from Long Eaton United in March 1977 for the bargain price of £5,000, although he had originally signed for Forest a couple of years earlier, playing one game, in the 2–0 home win against Hull City on 12 March 1977.

Birtles' first game since his return was at the City Ground in the 2–1 defeat of Arsenal on 9 September 1978; he didn't score but showed promise. His next game was to be an important one.

When the draw for the first round of the European Cup was made, large gasps of breath echoed across the Trent; Forest had been drawn to play the current holders of the trophy, the mighty Liverpool. A bit of extra spice came from the fact that Forest had beaten Liverpool to the title the previous season. At least the first leg would be at home. Forest fans weren't unduly worried as the Reds were proving to be something of a bogey-team for the 'Pool.

NOTTINGHAM FOREST 2–0 LIVERPOOL
European Cup, round one, first leg,
Wednesday 13 September 1978
Garry Birtles scored the opening goal for Forest, but as the game wore on there were lots of Forest fingernails chewed to the quick, then Colin Barrett made the game certain for the real Reds. Birtles headed a beautiful centre into the path of

the young full-back who let fly with a thunderous effort that crashed passed Clemence.

Forest: Shilton; Anderson, Barrett; McGovern, Lloyd, Burns; Gemmill, Bowyer, Birtles, Woodcock, Robertson
Scorers for Forest: Birtles, Barrett

LIVERPOOL 0–0 NOTTINGHAM FOREST
European Cup, round one, second leg,
Wednesday 27 September 1978
There was still a lot to do to win this tie, but Forest's rearguard proved equal to the task.
Forest: Shilton; Anderson, Clark; McGovern, Lloyd, Burns; Gemmill, Bowyer, Birtles, Woodcock, Robertson
Result: Forest won 2–0 on aggregate

AEK ATHENS 1–2 NOTTINGHAM FOREST
European Cup, round two, first leg,
Wednesday 18 October 1978
Gary Birtles came up with the goods once again. This time, John McGovern scored as well, although Athens also found the net.
Forest: Shilton; Anderson, Clark; McGovern, Lloyd, Burns; Gemmill, Bowyer, Birtles, Woodcock, Robertson
Scorers for Forest: McGovern, Birtles

NOTTINGHAM FOREST 5–1 AEK ATHENS
European Cup, round two, second leg,
Wednesday 1 November 1978
Birtles got his fourth and fifth European goals.
Forest: Shilton; Anderson, Clark; O'Hare, Lloyd, Needham; Gemmill, Bowyer, Birtles, Woodcock, Robertson; sub used: Mills (came on for Clark)
Result: Forest won 7–2 on aggregate
Scorers for Forest: Needham, Woodcock, Anderson, Birtles (2)

In February 1979, Brian Clough finally got his million-pound man – Trevor Francis. Cloughie had already told him to take his hands out of his pockets on national television when he presented the Birmingham City wonder boy with an award. Unfortunately, under UEFA rules Francis wasn't eligible to play in European competition until three months after his transfer. Elsewhere, on 26 February, Arsenal knocked Forest out of the FA Cup 1–0 in their fifth round clash at the City Ground.

NOTTINGHAM FOREST 4–1 GRASSHOPPERS ZURICH
European Cup, quarter-final, first leg,
Wednesday 7 March 1979
Birtles got his customary European goal, what a find this lad was proving to be!
Forest: Shilton; Anderson, Clark; McGovern, Lloyd, Needham; O'Neill, Gemmill, Birtles, Woodcock, Robertson
Scorers for Forest: Birtles, Robertson (penalty), Gemmill, Lloyd

On 17 March 1979, Nottingham Forest retained the League Cup, beating Southampton 3–2 in a thrilling final at Wembley.

GRASSHOPPERS ZURICH 1–1 NOTTINGHAM FOREST
European Cup, quarter-final, second leg,
Wednesday 21 March 1979
For once Birtles didn't score, but Martin O'Neill did.
Forest: Shilton; Anderson, Barrett; McGovern, Lloyd, Needham; O'Neill, Gemmill, Birtles, Woodcock, Robertson
Result: Forest won 5–2 on aggregate
Scorer for Forest: O'Neill

NOTTINGHAM FOREST 3–3 FC COLOGNE
European Cup, semi-final, first leg,
Wednesday 11 April 1979
Birtles got his customary European goal.
Forest: Shilton; Barrett, Bowyer; McGovern, Lloyd,
Needham; O'Neill, Gemmill, Birtles, Woodcock, Robertson
Scorers for Forest: Birtles, Bowyer, Robertson

FC COLOGNE 0–1 NOTTINGHAM FOREST
European Cup, semi-final, second leg,
Wednesday 25 April 1979
Amazingly, once again Birtles didn't score.
Forest: Shilton; Anderson, Clark; McGovern, Lloyd, Burns;
O'Neill, Bowyer, Birtles, Woodcock, Robertson
Result: Forest won 4–3 on aggregate
Scorer for Forest: Bowyer

Forest went into the final of the European Cup to face
Swedish champions Malmö FF, managed by Englishman Bob
Houghton, and coached by Keith Blunt. Houghton had been
recruited in January 1974, and under his tutelage Malmö had
won the Swedish Championship three times – 1974, 1975 and
1977. They had also been runners-up in 1976 and 1978, and
had won the Swedish Cup three times – 1974, 1975 and 1977
– making them three-time winners of the Swedish 'double'.
Despite Malmö's excellent domestic track record, Forest
were hopeful; their form leading up to the final was excellent.
Apart from a 1–0 defeat at Wolves on 4 April, Forest hadn't
lost a league game since 13 January. Following the Wolves
game they had drawn 1 and won 4 of the final 5 games of
the season. Malmö, on the other hand, had only won 1 of
their final 4 league games, drawing 2 and losing the other 1–0
away to Norrköping.

NOTTINGHAM FOREST 1–0 MALMÖ

European Cup final, the Olympic Stadium, Munich,
Wednesday 30 May 1979

Forest were pretty much at full strength, with Clough leaving out O'Neill and Gemmill, bringing in the now-eligible Trevor Francis for his first European game for Forest. The part-timers from Malmö, on the other hand, would be without a number of their star players. Midfield general 34-year-old Bo Larsson, Sweden's most capped player, needed an operation on his knee, while defenders Roy Andersson and Krister Kristensson would also be missing from the starting line-up. Then, on the eve of the final, Malmö captain Staffan Tapper broke his toe in training, but amazingly would still play. On their way to the final, Malmö had beaten Monaco, Dynamo Kiev, Wisła Kraków and Austria Vienna.

The game itself was a tense affair with Malmö packing their defence, and Forest throwing all they had at them. Then came a moment of magic as on the left wing, John Robertson beat two opponents before swinging over a marvellous cross that Trevor Francis stooped to head into the roof of the net. The game was effectively over, and, with the end result not in doubt, only the number of goals Forest would win by was still unresolved. Garry Birtles and Robbo missed reasonably good second-half chances, but fortunately that was not to matter. Forest had won the European Cup with a fabulous goal.

Forest: Shilton; Anderson, Clark; McGovern, Lloyd, Burns; Francis, Bowyer, Birtles, Woodcock, Robertson

Scorer for Forest: Francis

Forest had won the European Cup! Fan-bloody-tastic! Seeing John McGovern lift this wonderful, and very large, trophy above his head must have sent shivers of joy through every true supporter of Nottingham Forest. Football fans throughout our nation were thrilled for the club, the players, and of course, for Brian Clough and Peter Taylor.

Forest almost did the treble in 1978/79; however, they had to settle for the runners-up spot in the league, 8 points behind champions Liverpool. Forest drew 6 of their first 7 league games (and really should have won at least 4 of them), and in all drew 18 games in the course of the season, 9 of them 0–0. Once again the defence had performed admirably, only conceding 2 goals more than in the Championship-winning season. The problem was that they didn't score enough goals; their total of 61 was 9 less than 1977/78, compared to Liverpool who scored 85, and conceded only 16. Mind you, a 'double' of European Cup and Football League Cup was a marvellous achievement – one to be really proud of.

The 1979/80 European Cup

As holders of the European Championship, Forest had to defend their crown in this the 25th anniversary competition. Clough had signed a number of new players, including Asa Hartford and Frank Gray. Forest opened up the league campaign with 4 straight wins, was this going to be another Championship-winning season? Of the next 2 games, 1 was drawn, and in the other, Forest were beaten 3–1 away to Norwich. Oh, and Forest had beaten Blackburn 7–2 on aggregate in the League Cup.

NOTTINGHAM FOREST 2–0 ÖSTERS VÄXJÖ IF
European Cup, round one, first leg,
Wednesday 19 September 1979
A disappointingly low turnout considering the excitement of the previous season.
Forest: Shilton; Anderson, Gray; McGovern, Lloyd, Burns; O'Neill, Bowyer, Birtles, Woodcock, Robertson
Scorer for Forest: Bowyer (2)

ÖSTERS VÄXJÖ IF 1–1 NOTTINGHAM FOREST
European Cup, round one, second leg,
Wednesday 3 October 1979
Clough brought in young Gary Mills for his first European game. Tony Woodcock scored his first European goal.
Forest: Shilton; Anderson, Gray; McGovern, Lloyd, Burns; O'Neill, Mills, Birtles, Woodcock, Robertson; sub used: Bowyer (came on for O'Neill)
Result: Forest won 3–1 on aggregate
Scorer for Forest: Woodcock

NOTTINGHAM FOREST 2–0 FC ARGES PITESTI
European Cup, round two, first leg,
Wednesday 24 October 1979
Another disappointingly low gate saw Forest ease through this tie with a 2–0 home victory.
Forest: Shilton; Anderson, Gray; McGovern, Lloyd, Burns; Mills, Bowyer, Birtles, Woodcock, Robertson
Scorers for Forest: Woodcock, Birtles

FC ARGES PITESTI 1–2 NOTTINGHAM FOREST
European Cup, round two, second leg,
Wednesday 7 November 1979
John O'Hare played wide right.
Forest: Shilton; Anderson, Gray; McGovern, Lloyd, Burns; O'Hare, Bowyer, Birtles, Woodcock, Robertson; subs used: Gunn (came on for Gray), Mills (came on for O'Hare)
Result: Forest won 4–1 on aggregate
Scorers for Forest: Bowyer, Birtles

Forest now had to wait until March 1980 for the third round games. In the league, things had taken a turn for the worse. From 13 October 1979, Forest lost 7 out of their next 10 league games – 6 of these were away, drawing 1, and winning only twice; both times at home in this disastrous period. Aside from notching 5 against Bolton, Forest were finding it difficult to score, especially away from the City Ground. Cloughie had a few surprises up his sleeve, transfer-wise. First in November 1979, he sold Tony Woodcock to Bundesliga side Cologne. The superbly talented Stan Bowles arrived at the City Ground in December 1979, then the unpredictable Charlie George was signed in January 1980. Incidentally, he arrived in time to line up against Barcelona in the European Super Cup, because the 1979/89 final had to be played early in 1980 as neither Forest or FC Barcelona could sort out suitable dates for the two-legged match.

NOTTINGHAM FOREST 1–0 FC BARCELONA
European Super Cup, first leg, Wednesday 30 January 1980
A confident Barça side arrived in Nottingham as winners of the UEFA Cup Winners' Cup, but it was Forest that took the lead early on in the first leg at the City Ground, with Charlie George scoring after 9 minutes. Forest's defence held firm to prevent Barcelona from scoring.
Forest: Shilton; Anderson, Gray; O'Neill, Lloyd, Burns; Francis, Bowyer, Birtles, George, Robertson
Scorer for Forest: George

FC BARCELONA 1–1 NOTTINGHAM FOREST
European Super Cup, second leg, Tuesday 5 February 1980
Stan Bowles came in for his first European game for Forest. Barcelona squared the tie in the 25th minute, when Carlos Roberto beat Peter Shilton from the penalty spot, but 3 minutes before half-time Kenny Burns equalised to restore Forest's lead. Forest held on to draw the game 1–1 and win the UEFA Super Cup with a 2–1 aggregate victory. Not many teams got a result at the Nou Camp.
Forest: Shilton; Anderson, Gray; McGovern, Lloyd, Burns; Francis, Bowles, Birtles, George, Robertson; sub used: O'Neill (came on for Francis)
Result: Forest won 2–1 on aggregate
Scorer for Forest: Burns

What a fantastic haul of trophies Clough and Taylor, and their teams, were bringing to the City Ground; multiple League Cups, the League Championship, the European Cup, and now the European Super Cup – incredible! They were back in European Cup action a month later.

NOTTINGHAM FOREST 0–1 DYNAMO BERLIN
European Cup, quarter-final, first leg,
Wednesday 5 March 1980
The unthinkable happened! Not only did Forest fail to win 2–0, but actually failed to score a goal, and lost at home for the first time in this competition.
Forest: Shilton; Gunn, Gray; McGovern, Lloyd, Burns; O'Neill, Bowles, Birtles, Francis, Robertson

Before the second leg of this quarter-final tie, Forest had another date at Wembley, to play Wolves in the final of the League Cup, which as we know, Forest had won in the two previous seasons. The Reds were odds-on favourites to land the trophy for the third successive time. Unfortunately, on Saturday 15 March 1980, that fickle old 'Dame Fate' had other ideas, as Forest went down 1–0 to a somewhat jammy Andy Gray goal.
Forest: Shilton; Anderson, Gray; McGovern, Needham, Burns; O'Neill, Bowyer, Birtles, Francis, Robertson

Four days later, Forest were in Berlin for the second leg of the European Cup quarter-final, hoping to be able to overturn Berlin's single-goal advantage.

DYNAMO BERLIN 1–3 NOTTINGHAM FOREST
European Cup, quarter-final, second leg,
Wednesday 19 March 1980
As it turned out there was no need to worry. Forest produced some quality football to win through to the semi-final of this competition. Dave Needham got his first European game of

the season, and Trevor Francis grabbed a brace in a fantastic performance, one of the greatest recoveries since Lazarus!
Forest: Shilton; Anderson, Gray; McGovern, Lloyd, Needham; O'Neill, Bowyer, Birtles, Francis, Robertson
Result: Forest won 3–2 on aggregate
Scorers for Forest: Francis (2), Robertson (penalty)

NOTTINGHAM FOREST 2–0 AJAX

European Cup, semi-final, first leg, Wednesday 9 April 1980
Back on to the 2–0 track!
Forest: Shilton; Anderson, Gray; McGovern, Lloyd, Burns; O'Neill, Bowles, Birtles, Francis, Robertson
Scorers for Forest: Francis, Robertson (penalty)

AJAX 1–0 NOTTINGHAM FOREST

European Cup, semi-final, second leg,
Wednesday 23 April 1980
Forest: Shilton; Anderson, Gray; McGovern, Lloyd, Burns; O'Neill, Bowyer, Birtles, Francis, Robertson
Result: Forest won 2–1 on aggregate

Forest were into the final of the European Cup for the second year in a row. This time, Forest would face German champions Hamburg, and their star player, the enigmatic, Brut-drenched, curly-permed Kevin Keegan. Back in the league, Forest failed to win any of their final 7 away games, and it was this poor away form that cost them a chance of winning the league title for a second time. Oh well! What a pity . . . never mind, there was still the European Cup to aim for. Sadly, Trevor Francis had injured his achilles tendon in April, and wouldn't be fit for the final; actually he didn't play again until December, the following season. Hamburg would also be without star striker Horst Hrubesch, although he did make the subs' bench.

NOTTINGHAM FOREST 1–0 SV HAMBURG
European Cup final, the Bernabeu, Madrid,
Wednesday 28 May 1980

For this match Clough selected Martin O'Neill in place of the injured Francis, and Gary Mills started as partner to Garry Birtles. This time it was Forest who adopted a defensive attitude, drawing Hamburg on to them, but the nearest the Germans came to a goal was when Magath forced Peter Shilton to push his free-kick past the post. Then, in a rare upfield foray, a lovely exchange of passes between Garry Birtles and John Robertson saw Robbo move inside to hit a low right-foot shot past Hamburg keeper Kargus' left hand to cannon into the net off the inside of the post. Hamburg had a goal given offside, but subsequent attacks were well repulsed by Forest's stoic defence. And then it was over – Forest had retained the trophy.

Forest: Shilton; Anderson, Gray; McGovern, Lloyd, Burns; O'Neill, Bowyer, Birtles, Mills, Robertson; subs used: Gunn (came on for Gray), O'Hare (came on for Mills)
Scorer for Forest: Robertson

Nottingham Forest had now won two European Cups! John McGovern proudly lifted the huge trophy for the second time, once again sending Forest fans into flights of ecstasy. Another great season, which, but for a little more luck, might have been even more successful if Forest hadn't lost so many away games.

1979/80 final top six league placings:

	Pld	W	D	L	F	A	W	D	L	F	A	Pts
Liverpool	42	15	6	0	46	8	10	4	7	35	22	60
Man Utd	42	17	3	1	43	8	7	7	7	22	27	58
Ipswich	42	14	4	3	43	13	8	5	8	25	26	53
Arsenal	42	8	10	3	24	12	10	6	5	28	24	52
Forest	42	16	4	1	44	11	4	4	13	19	32	48
Wolves	42	9	6	6	29	20	10	3	8	29	27	47

The 1980/81 European Cup

The Reds would again compete in the European Cup; once again as holders. Could Forest make it a hat-trick? Unfortunately, the team was breaking up a little; also some players were getting on a bit. Clough signed a number of new players, including Swiss international Raimondo Ponte (who stayed one season, making 24 appearances plus 8 as substitute, scoring 7 goals), and free-scoring Ian Wallace from Coventry. In his first season the young Scot managed 11 goals in 37 league games, plus 3 in cup competitions.

Forest lost 2 of their first league games, obviously, it wasn't going to be a cake-walk to the title. A bad omen, Forest had been drawn away for the first leg of round one, the first time this had happened in this competition.

CSKA SOFIA 1–0 NOTTINGHAM FOREST

European Cup, round one, first leg,
Wednesday 17 September 1980
Forest's team for this first European Cup game had a familiar ring to it; more out of expediency than choice.
Forest: Shilton; Anderson, Gray; McGovern, Lloyd, Needham; O'Neill, Bowyer, Birtles, Wallace, Robertson;
sub used: Ponte (came on for Wallace)

NOTTINGHAM FOREST 0–1 CSKA SOFIA

European Cup, round one, second leg,
Wednesday 1 October 1980
Oh dear. No matter what Forest threw at CSKA, they just couldn't score.
Forest: Shilton; Anderson, Gray; McGovern, Needham, Burns; O'Neill, Bowyer, Birtles, Wallace, Robertson;
sub used: Lloyd (came on for Burns)
Result: Forest lost 2–0 on aggregate

And that, as they say, was that! Twenty-two games in this competition, 12 won, 4 drawn and 4 lost, makes a pretty damned good record. Before Forest finished with Europe that season, they had the European Super Cup to defend.

NOTTINGHAM FOREST 2–1 VALENCIA CF
European Super Cup Final, first leg,
Tuesday 25 November 1980

Forest became the first club to play two European Super Cup finals in the same year, having beaten FC Barcelona back in January. Valencia got that vital away goal, when Dario Luis Felman opened the scoring for the visitors 2 minutes after half time. Then, in the 57th minute, Ian Bowyer equalised for the home side, before adding a second one minute from time.

Forest: Shilton; Anderson, Gray; McGovern, Lloyd, Burns; Mills, Bowyer, Ward, Wallace, Robertson; sub used: Ponte (came on for Ward)

Scorer for Forest: Bowyer (2)

CF VALENCIA 1–0 NOTTINGHAM FOREST
European Super Cup Final, second leg,
Wednesday 17 December 1980

At the Luis Casanova stadium, Valencia became the first team to win the final on the away goals rule. Forest tried hard but couldn't find a goal to cancel out Fernando Morena's 51st-minute strike.

Forest: Shilton; Anderson, Gunn; McGovern, Lloyd, Burns; O'Neill, Ponte, Francis, Wallace, Walsh.

Result: Forest drew 2–2 on aggregate, but lost on away goals.

The 1983/84 UEFA Cup

Forest had to wait a couple of years for their next tilt at a European title; this time it was in the UEFA Cup, which Forest had competed in twice before under its old name of the Inter-Cities Fairs Cup. A fifth-place finish in the league in 1982/83 was what earned the Reds this opportunity.

The Forest team had taken on an altogether different look. Gone were Peter Shilton, Frank Gray, John McGovern, Larry

Lloyd, Kenny Burns, Dave Needham, Martin O'Neill, Trevor Francis and John Robertson, but at least Garry Birtles was back from Manchester United and Viv Anderson had rejoined in February 1983. Forest were drawn at home for the first leg in round one, but unfortunately it wasn't home as Forest fans know it. This first leg was ordered to be played on a so-called neutral ground at Oder, on the East German/Polish border – how that could be neutral, I have no idea. Never mind, Forest won, that's all that mattered.

NOTTINGHAM FOREST 2–0 FC VORWAERTS
UEFA Cup, round one, first leg,
Wednesday 14 September 1983
Forest: van Breukelen; Anderson, Swain; Todd, Fairclough, Bowyer; Walsh, Wallace, Davenport, Hodge, Wigley; sub used: Gunn (came on for Davenport)
Scorers for Forest: Wallace, Hodge

FC VORWAERTS 0–1 NOTTINGHAM FOREST
UEFA Cup, round one, second leg,
Wednesday 28 September 1983
Forest: van Breukelen; Anderson, Swain; Todd, Hart, Bowyer; Wigley, Wallace, Birtles, Hodge, Walsh; subs used: Gunn (came on for Swain), Wilson (came on for Walsh)
Result: Forest won 3–0 on aggregate
Scorer for Forest: Bowyer

PSV EINDHOVEN 1–2 NOTTINGHAM FOREST
UEFA Cup, round two, first leg,
Wednesday 19 October 1983
Forest: van Breukelen; Anderson, Swain; Todd, Hart, Bowyer; Wigley, Wallace, Davenport, Walsh, Hodge; sub used: Fairclough (came on for Hodge)
Scorers for Forest: Davenport, Walsh (penalty)

NOTTINGHAM FOREST 1–0 PSV EINDHOVEN
UEFA Cup, round two, second leg,
Wednesday 2 November 1983
Somehow, this tie failed to capture the imagination of the
Nottingham public.
Forest: Sutton; Anderson, Swain; Todd, Hart, Bowyer;
Wigley, Wallace, Davenport, Walsh, Hodge; subs used:
Fairclough (came on for Wigley), Birtles (came on for
Wallace)
Result: Forest won 3–1 on aggregate
Scorer for Forest: Davenport

A game hailed as a contender for the British Championship,
between two former winners of the European Cup followed
next.

NOTTINGHAM FOREST 0–0 CELTIC
UEFA Cup, round three, first leg,
Wednesday 23 November 1983
A large number of Scotsmen invaded Nottingham to watch
their favourites take on the Reds.
Forest: Sutton; Anderson, Swain; Fairclough, Hart, Bowyer;
Wigley, Davenport, Birtles, Hodge, Walsh; sub used: Wallace
(came on for Davenport)

CELTIC 1–2 NOTTINGHAM FOREST
UEFA Cup, round three, second leg,
Wednesday 7 December 1983
Forest: van Breukelen; Anderson, Swain; Fairclough, Hart,
Bowyer; Wigley, Davenport, Birtles, Walsh, Hodge
Result: Forest won 2–1 on aggregate
Scorers for Forest: Hodge, Walsh

NOTTINGHAM FOREST 1–0 RAIKA STURM GRAZ
UEFA Cup, quarter-final, first leg,
Wednesday 7 March 1984
Forest: van Breukelen; Anderson, Swain; Fairclough, Hart,
Bowyer; Wigley, Wallace, Birtles, Hodge, Walsh; subs used:
Gunn (came on for Anderson), Davenport (came on for Walsh)
Scorer for Forest: Hart

RAIKA STURM GRAZ 1–1 NOTTINGHAM FOREST
UEFA Cup, quarter-final, second leg,
Wednesday 21 March 1984
Forest: van Breukelen; Anderson, Swain; Fairclough, Hart,
Bowyer; Thijssen, Davenport, Birtles, Hodge, Walsh
Result: Forest won 3–1 on aggregate
Scorer for Forest: Walsh (penalty)

NOTTINGHAM FOREST 2 v ANDERLECHT 0
UEFA Cup, semi-final, first leg,
Wednesday 11 April 1984
Forest: van Breukelen; Anderson, Swain; Fairclough, Hart,
Bowyer; Wigley, Mills, Davenport, Hodge, Walsh
Result: Forest won 2–0
Scorer for Forest: Hodge 2

ANDERLECHT 3–0 NOTTINGHAM FOREST
UEFA Cup, semi-final, second leg,
Wednesday 25 April 1984
Well flippin' 'eck! How did Forest lose this tie? The referee
awarded Anderlecht a dodgy penalty, then disallowed a good
Forest goal. 'Fixed!' was the cry. It certainly was a night filled
with strange decisions.
Forest: van Breukelen; Anderson, Swain; Fairclough, Hart,
Bowyer; Wigley, Mills, Davenport, Hodge, Walsh; sub used:
Birtles (came on for Hodge)
Result: Forest lost 3–2 on aggregate

The result of this tie was subsequently the subject of an investigation by UEFA amid allegations of bribery and match-fixing. In the end, UEFA decided that the result would stand. It was no consolation to Forest that Anderlecht later admitted that there had been a number of indiscretions; an understatement if ever there was one. Anderlecht made it to the final, where they were beaten 4–3 on penalties by Tottenham Hotspur after both legs had been drawn 1–1 – cheats never prosper!

It was later reported that Nottingham Forest plus a number of former players had begun court proceedings against Anderlecht, one of Belgium's largest football clubs, over the 1984 UEFA Cup bribery scandal, following allegations that in 1997 the former chairman of the Belgian club admitted that the referee was paid the equivalent of £27,000 as a 'loan' ahead of the semi-final second leg.

Forest finished a creditable third in the league, behind Liverpool and Southampton, to qualify for the UEFA Cup. The 1983/84 final top three league placings looked like this:

	Pld	W	D	L	F	A	W	D	L	F	A	Pts
Liverpool	42	14	5	2	50	12	8	9	4	23	20	80
So'ton	42	15	4	2	44	17	7	7	7	22	21	77
Forest	42	14	4	3	47	17	8	4	9	29	28	74

The 1984/85 UEFA Cup
Unfortunately, this excursion into Europe was destined to be a short-lived affair.

NOTTINGHAM FOREST 0–0 CLUB BRUGGE KV
UEFA Cup, round one, first leg,
Wednesday 19 September 1984
Not a very good start to this campaign.
Forest: Sutton; Gunn, Swain; Fairclough, Smalley, Bowyer; Wigley, Metgod, Christie, Davenport, Walsh; sub used: Mills (came on for Christie)

CLUB BRUGGE KV 1–0 NOTTINGHAM FOREST
UEFA Cup, round one, second leg,
Wednesday 3 October 1984
Forest: Sutton; Gunn, Swain; Fairclough, Hart, Bowyer;
Mills, Metgod, Christie, Davenport, Hodge
Result: Forest lost 1–0 on aggregate

No one would have guessed that this would be Forest's last
European appearance for a decade. Heartbreaking scenes
were witnessed at the Heysel Stadium in Brussels on 29 May
1985, when the fans of Liverpool and Juventus clashed with
disastrous results; thirty-eight people died, and more than 400
suffered injuries of one sort or another. The appalling scenes
were beamed around the world by television companies,
whose audiences had tuned in expecting to see an exciting
European Cup final. Somewhat surprisingly, the game went
ahead, Juventus winning 1–0 with a Michel Platini penalty.

The disaster had various consequences, the Belgian
government was brought down, and within days of the
tragedy the Football Association indefinitely withdrew all
English clubs from European competition for one year.
UEFA decided that this was an insufficient punishment and
slapped an indefinite ban on all English clubs, with Liverpool
receiving an extra three-year ban once English clubs were
allowed back into Europe.

Six English clubs qualified for European competitions
in the following season (1985/86). Four of these, Everton,
Manchester United, Norwich and Southampton, considered
the ban to be unfair as they had not been involved at Heysel,
taking their claims to the High Court hoping to have the ban
lifted. Liverpool decided to proceed with independent legal
action. Only Tottenham decided not to be involved. The clubs
failed to have the UEFA decision overturned, the judge ruling
against their petition.

In 1986, FIFA lifted its ban on English clubs playing overseas
friendlies, but in May UEFA decided against readmitting

English clubs into European competitions. The situation was not helped when, at the 1988 European Championships in Germany, hordes of English supporters ran amok.

The ban was to have the effect of preventing Nottingham Forest from competing in the UEFA Cup in 1987/88, 1988/89 and 1989/90. On 18 April 1990, UEFA finally ended the five-season exile of English clubs, providing that English fans behaved themselves at the forthcoming World Cup finals (Liverpool would be banned for one more season).

Manchester United made a triumphant return to European competition by beating Barcelona to win the European Cup Winners' Cup in 1990/91. Only one English club was allowed to compete in the UEFA Cup – Aston Villa as Division One runners-up – not good news for Forest who had won the League Cup and should surely have been allowed to enter the competition. On a sad note for Forest, Peter Taylor died on 5 October 1990. He was only 62 years old.

It was to be another five years before Forest qualified for a European competition.

The 1995/96 UEFA Cup
A third-place finish in the First Division in 1994/95 gained Forest entry into this competition, following their (new) Division One runners-up spot the season before. It was to be a bit better than last time, but unfortunately, not like the old halcyon days under Cloughie. At least one of Brian's old boys, Frank Clark, was now manager. Forest faced their old adversaries Malmö, now coached by Rolf Zetterlund.

MALMÖ FF 2–1 NOTTINGHAM FOREST
UEFA Cup, round one, first leg,
Tuesday 12 September 1995
Malmö played a 4-5-1 formation. Things began to look good for Forest when Ian Woan scored in the 36th minute, but on 58 minutes, Joakim Persson equalised for the home side. Then 14 minutes later Anders Andersson netted the winner for Malmö.

Forest: Crossley; Lyttle, Pearce; Cooper, Chettle, Phillips; Stone, Gemmill, Roy, Campbell, Woan; subs used: Bart-Williams (came on for Pearce), Lee (came on for Campbell)
Scorer for Forest: Woan

NOTTINGHAM FOREST 1–0 MALMÖ FF

UEFA Cup, round one, second leg,

Tuesday 26 September 1995

Bryan Roy got the goal that took Forest into the next round in the 69th minute.

Forest: Crossley; Lyttle, Pearce; Cooper, Chettle, Bart-Williams; Stone, Bohinen, Roy, Lee, Woan; subs used: Gemmill (came on for Bohinen), Silenzi (came on for Roy)
Result: Forest drew 2–2 on aggregate and went through on the away goals rule
Scorer for Forest: Roy

AUXERRE 0–1 NOTTINGHAM FOREST

UEFA Cup, round two, first leg,

Tuesday 17 October 1995

Forest: Crossley; Lyttle, Pearce; Cooper, Chettle, Bart-Williams; Stone, Gemmill, Haaland, Lee, Woan; sub used: Silenzi (came on for Lee)
Scorer for Forest: Stone

NOTTINGHAM FOREST 0–0 AUXERRE

UEFA Cup, round two, second leg,

Tuesday 31 October 1995

Forest: Crossley; Lyttle, Pearce; Cooper, Chettle, Bart-Williams; Stone, Gemmill, Roy, Lee, Woan; subs used: Haaland (came on for Gemmill), McGregor (came on for Roy)
Result: Forest won 1–0 on aggregate

NOTTINGHAM FOREST 1–0 LYON
UEFA Cup, round three, first leg,
Tuesday 21 November 1995
Forest: Crossley; Lyttle, Pearce; Cooper, Chettle, Bart-Williams; Stone, Gemmill, Roy, Silenzi, Woan; subs used: McGregor (came on for Roy), Howe (came on for Silenzi)
Scorer for Forest: McGregor

LYON 0–0 NOTTINGHAM FOREST
UEFA Cup, round three, second leg,
Tuesday 5 December 1995
Forest: Crossley; Lyttle, Pearce; Cooper, Chettle, Bart-Williams; Stone, Gemmill, Howe, Lee, Woan; subs used: Haaland (came on for Gemmill), Silenzi (came on for Lee)
Result: Forest won 1–0 on aggregate

BAYERN MUNICH 2–1 NOTTINGHAM FOREST
UEFA Cup, quarter-final, first leg,
Tuesday 5 March 1996
Forest: Crossley; Phillips, Pearce; Haaland, Chettle, Bart-Williams; Stone, Gemmill, Roy, Campbell, Woan
Scorer for Forest: Chettle

NOTTINGHAM FOREST 1–5 BAYERN MUNICH
UEFA Cup, quarter-final, second leg,
Tuesday 19 March 1996
Yes, Forest lost 5–1. Jurgen Klinsmann bagged a brace to go with his goal from the first leg.
Forest: Crossley; Lyttle, Pearce; Cooper, Chettle, Bart-Williams; Stone, Phillips, Roy, Campbell, Woan; subs used: Haaland (came on for Lyttle), McGregor (came on for Bart-Williams), Silenzi (came on for Campbell)
Result: Forest lost 7–2 on aggregate
Scorer for Forest: Stone

Well, what a way to tumble out of this competition! It was the last time (to date) that Nottingham Forest would compete in a European competition.

CLOUGHIE ON THE BECKHAMS

'Beckham? His wife can't sing and his barber can't cut hair.'
Cloughie's comment about Posh and Becks

'He should guide Posh in the direction of a singing coach because she's nowhere near as good at her job as her husband.'
Cloughie's advice to Becks

'Who the hell wants 14 pairs of shoes when you go on holiday? I haven't had 14 pairs in my life!'
Cloughie's view on the contents of Posh's missing luggage

FA CUP – FOREST'S SEMI-FINALS

Nottingham Forest have appeared in twelve semi-finals of the FA Cup, winning three, but losing nine. In the first round of the 1878/79 English FA Challenge Cup, Forest made their debut against neighbours Notts County at the Beeston Cricket Ground (the Magpies' home ground at the time). The rules of the competition stipulated that an entrance fee be paid by all spectators, and over 500 turned up to watch Forest win the game 3–1. In round two, Forest beat Sheffield FC 2–0 at home, while in round three they beat Old Harrovians 2–0 at home, then Oxford University 2–1 at home in the quarter-final, going on to reach the semi-final. However, they were then to be beaten 2–1 by Old Etonians, the eventual winners of the competition, at Kennington Oval.

One year later, in 1879/80, Forest again reached the semi-finals, having beaten Notts County 4–0 at home in round one. In round two Forest beat Turton FC from Lancashire 6–0 away, then in round three they beat Blackburn Rovers 6–0 at home. In round five the Reds drew 2–2 at home to Sheffield FC, but won the tie when Sheffield were disqualified. Forest received a bye in the quarter-finals, but went down 1–0 to Oxford University in the semi-final at Kennington Oval.

A third semi-final appearance came in 1884/85. In round one Forest beat Rotherham 5–0 at home, then in round two they beat Heeley FC from Sheffield 4–1 at home. In round three Forest beat Sheffield Wednesday 2–1 away, then in round four beat Swifts FC from Slough 1–0 away. In the fifth round Forest received a bye, then went on to beat Old Etonians 2–0 away. In the semi-final Forest were drawn away to face the Scottish aces from Glasgow, Queens Park. The first game, played on a neutral ground – the Racecourse Ground in Derby – ended in a 1–1 draw, but in the replay Forest were again beaten, this time 3–0, the match being played at Merchiston Castle School grounds in Colinton village near Edinburgh (the castle was once the home of John Napier, the inventor of logarithms).

In the 1891/92 FA Cup competition, Forest reached a fourth semi-final. Round one saw them beat Newcastle 2–1 at home. In round two Forest beat Sunderland 1–0 away, and in round three beat Preston 2–0 at home. The semi-final against West Bromwich Albion proved to be a long, drawn-out affair. The first game, at Molineux, ended 1–1, as did the replay, again at Molineux. However, Forest lost the second replay, played at the Racecourse Ground at Derby, 6–2.

Forest had become champions of the Football Alliance in 1891/92, and were set to join the Football League for the next season when Division One was increased from fourteen to sixteen clubs.

Forest were successful in the semis of the FA Cup in 1897/98 and went on to win the final (see p. 59 for details of this campaign).

Forest next reached the FA Cup semi-finals in 1899/1900. In round one they beat Grimsby 3–0 at home, and in round two beat Sunderland 2–0 at home. In round three they beat Preston 1–0 at home, to reach the semi-finals where they were drawn to play Bury at the Victoria Ground, Stoke. The game ended 1–1 and sadly Forest lost the replay at Bramall Lane 3–2 .

In the 1901/02 FA Cup, Forest won through to their seventh semi-final. In round one they beat Glossop 3–1 away, and in round two Manchester City 2–0 away. In round three Forest beat Stoke 2–0 at home, only to lose the semi-final 3–1 to Southampton at White Hart Lane.

The Reds were successful in their 1958/59 FA Cup campaign, the details of which are on p. 60.

Forest's next losing FA Cup semi-final came in 1966/67 when, after winning 2–1 at Plymouth Argyle in round three, 3–0 at home to Newcastle in round four, 3–0 at home to Swindon in round five and beating Everton 3–2 at home in the sixth round, they lost the semi-final 2–1 to Tottenham Hotspur at Hillsborough.

Nottingham Forest hearts were broken again in 1987/88. After beating Halifax 4–0 away in round three, Leyton Orient 2–1 away in round four, Birmingham City 1–0 away in round five and Arsenal 2–1 away in the sixth round, Forest were drawn to play Liverpool in the semi-finals at Hillsborough, losing 2–1. Liverpool lost the final 1–0 to Wimbledon.

One season later, in 1988/89, came the semi-final everyone in football would want to forget. Forest had beaten Ipswich 3–0 at home in round three, then Leeds 2–0 at home, then Watford 3–0 away, and Manchester United 1–0 away in the sixth round. In a repeat of the previous season, Forest were drawn to play Liverpool in the semi-final at Hillsborough. The game was abandoned after 6 minutes when it became obvious that Liverpool fans in the Leppings Lane end of the ground were being crushed against the barrier surrounding the pitch; a tragedy (see p. 87). The game eventually went ahead at Old Trafford, Liverpool winning 3–1.

Nottingham Forest's twelfth and last appearance in an FA Cup semi-final (1990/91) ended happily when Forest triumphed 4–0 over West Ham at Villa Park. Sadly they lost the final 2–1 to Tottenham Hotspur.

FOREST'S FA CUP VICTORIES

Nottingham Forest have won the FA Cup on two occasions: 1898 and 1959. They were also runners-up in 1991. Here are the details:

1898 FA Cup Campaign

Round	Opponent	Venue	Score
One	Grimsby Town	Home	4–0
Two	Gainsborough Trinity	Home	4–0
Three	West Bromwich Albion	Away	3–2
Semi-final	Southampton Town	Away	1–1
Semi-final replay	Southampton	Home	2–0
Final	Derby County	Crystal Palace	3–1

1898 FA Cup final

Success for Forest finally came in the 1898 FA Cup. The Reds won the semi-final, beating Southampton 2–0 after a 1–1 draw, then in the final at Crystal Palace on 16 April 1898, triumphing 3–1 over rivals Derby County. Forest's scorers were Capes (2) and McPherson, while Steve Bloomer scored for the Rams.

Teams

Nottingham Forest: Allsop; Ritchie, Scott; Forman (Frank), McPherson, Wragg; McInnes, Richards, Benbow, Capes, Spouncer

Derby County: Fryer; Methven, Leiper; Cox, Goodall A., Turner; Goodall J., Bloomer, Boag, Stevenson, McQueen

Sadly it was back to semi-final defeats again in 1900 when Bury beat Forest 3–2, and again in 1902 when the Reds were beaten 3–1 by Southampton. Then Forest hit a 57-year FA Cup slump until the glorious summer of 1959 when they won the FA Cup trophy for the second time, beating Luton Town 2–1 at Wembley on 2 May.

1959 FA Cup Campaign

Round	Opponent	Venue	Score
Three	Tooting & Mitcham Utd	Away	2–2
Three replay	Tooting & Mitcham Utd	Home	3–0
Four	Grimsby Town	Home	4–1
Five	Birmingham City	Away	1–1
Five replay	Birmingham City	Home	1–1
Five 2nd replay	Birmingham City	Filbert Street	5–0
Six	Bolton Wanderers	Home	2–1
Semi-final	Aston Villa	Hillsborough	1–0
Final	Luton Town	Wembley	2–1

1959 FA Cup Final

Nottingham Forest 2–1 Luton Town
Scorers for Forest: Dwight, Wilson
Scorer for Luton: Pacey
Attendance: 100,000   **Receipts:** £40,708

Forest went one up in the 9th minute when Roy Dwight converted Stewart Imlach's cross, and 5 minutes later grabbed a second through Tommy Wilson who headed home Billy Gray's centre. Forest were in total command until the 33rd minute when Roy Dwight broke his leg in a tackle with Luton's Brendan McNally. As no substitutes were allowed then, ten-man Forest held out until David Pacey clawed a goal back for the Hatters in the 62nd minute. The Reds managed to see out a nervy final 28 minutes to win the coveted trophy.

Nottingham Forest: Thomson; Whare, McDonald; Whitefoot, McKinlay, Burkitt; Dwight, Quigley, Wilson, Gray, Imlach
Luton Town: Baynham; McNally, Hawkes; Groves, Owen, Pacey; Bingham, Brown, Morton, Cummins, Gregory

THE FA CHARITY SHIELD (ALSO KNOWN AS THE FA COMMUNITY SHIELD)

The Reds were runners-up in the 1959 FA Charity Shield, beaten 4–1 by Wolves. However, they did win it at Wembley on 12 August 1978, inflicting a humiliating 5–0 defeat on Ipswich Town, with two goals from Martin O'Neill, and one each from Larry Lloyd, Peter Withe, and John Robertson.

Nottingham Forest: Shilton; Anderson, Barrett; McGovern, Lloyd, Burns; O'Neill (Needham), Gemmill A., Withe, Woodcock, Robertson

FAIR PLAY AWARD

Instigated by the PFA in 1988 to reward the club with the best disciplinary record throughout the Football League and the Premier League, the PFA Bobby Moore Fair Play Award was based upon penalty points accumulated for cautions and sendings-off. This allows the PFA to illuminate good behaviour and sportsmanship. It is named after Bobby Moore of West Ham and, of course, England (for whom he lifted the World Cup in 1966), and who was renowned for his fair play ethic. Liverpool have won it three times, while Crewe Alexandra have been awarded it twelve times. However, most importantly for us, Forest won this accolade in 1990/91.

LEAGUE CUP

Since 1982, the FA League Cup has been rebranded to include the name of its sponsor:

1982 to 1986 the competition was sponsored by the Milk Marketing Board and became known as the Milk Cup.
1986 to 1990 Littlewoods took over the sponsorship and the competition was renamed the Littlewoods Challenge Cup.
1990 to 1992 Rumbelows became the sponsor and so the competition was called the Rumbelows Cup.
1992 to 1998 Coca-Cola took over the sponsorship with the competition being named the Coca-Cola Cup.

So we'd had milk, football pools, electrical goods and soft drinks, but now the FA turned to beer producers for sponsorship:

1998 to 2003 Worthington took up the sponsorship of the competition.
2003 to the present day, Carling are the sponsors, hence the competition is now known as the Carling Cup.

Nottingham Forest's record in this competition is good, having won it on four separate occasions: 1978, 1979, 1989 and 1990. Only Wolves' narrow 1–0 victory in 1980 prevented a hat-trick of successive victories for Forest.

Forest have twice been runners-up in this competition – 1979/80 and 1991/92.

League Cup Wins
Liverpool hold the record for the highest number of League Cup victories with seven. Second are Aston Villa with five. Forest are third with four wins.

League Cup Successive Victories

Nottingham Forest successfully defended their League Cup title on two separate occasions: in 1978/79 having won the competition in 1977/78, and again in 1989/90 having won the competition in 1988/89. Only Manchester United (once), and Liverpool have achieved this feat, mind you Liverpool have also won the competition four years running.

FOREST'S LEAGUE CUP FINALS

1977/78 League Cup Final – Forest 1–0 Liverpool in the replay after a 0–0 draw

On their way to the League Championship in 1977/78, Brian Clough's unfashionable Nottingham Forest team met First Division rivals Liverpool at Wembley on 18 March in the League Cup final. Goalkeeper Peter Shilton was cup-tied having already turned out in the competition for Stoke City, so Cloughie drafted in 18-year-old Chris Woods, who produced an outstanding display on his way to keeping a clean sheet. Also ineligible were Archie Gemmill and Dave Needham.

John McGovern was injured during the game and was substituted, John O'Hare taking his place. Four days later, 22 March, in the replay at Old Trafford, Woods was again outstanding as he and his heroic team-mates held a star-studded Liverpool team. Forest won the game with a controversial John Robertson penalty after Phil Thompson had brought down John O'Hare.

Forest's winning team at Old Trafford: Chris Woods; Viv Anderson, Frank Clark; John O'Hare, Larry Lloyd, Kenny Burns; Martin O'Neill, Ian Bowyer, Peter Withe, Tony Woodcock, John Robertson

1978/79 League Cup final
Nottingham Forest 3–2 Southampton

Back at Wembley in the competition one year on, League Champions Nottingham Forest were still involved in four competitions: fighting it out for the First Division title with Liverpool, the European Cup, the FA Cup, plus the defence of their League Cup title. They had already despatched Oldham, Oxford, Everton, Brighton and, in the semi-final, Watford. This time Southampton were Forest's opponents. As a tribute to the part he had played in Nottingham Forest's success, Peter Taylor led the Forest team out onto the pitch. Cloughie had again confounded his critics by selling his star striker Peter Withe to Newcastle United earlier that season. In his place played ex-Long Eaton hero, Garry Birtles, who had proved an instant hit. Southampton scored first before half time, but then Garry Birtles scored two second-half goals to make the score 2–1. Tony Woodcock made it 3–1 to Forest, but then Southampton made it 3–2 to set up a nervy end to the game. Thankfully the Reds hung on to win the game and become the first team to successfully defend the League Cup title.

Forest's winning team: Peter Shilton; Colin Barrett, Frank Clark; John McGovern, Larry Lloyd, Dave Needham; Martin O'Neill, Archie Gemmill, Garry Birtles, Tony Woodcock, John Robertson

1988/89 League Cup final
Nottingham Forest 3–1 Luton Town

In a repeat of their 1959 FA Cup triumph, and ten years since their last League Cup final victory, Nottingham Forest reached Wembley to face Luton Town, after disposing of Chester, Coventry, Leicester, QPR and, in the semi-final, Bristol City. Luton were defending their League Cup victory of the previous season. A resilient Luton proved to be tough opposition and when Mick Harford scored with a header in the first half, Forest had to call upon all their stars to gain control of the game. A determined Forest began the second period strongly, winning a penalty when Steve Hodge was fouled by the Hatters' keeper, which Nigel Clough scored. Neil Webb gave Forest the lead before Nigel Clough scored again to make the score 3–1 to the Reds.

Forest's winning team: Steve Sutton; Brian Laws, Stuart Pearce; Des Walker, Terry Wilson, Steve Hodge; Tommy Gaynor, Neil Webb, Nigel Clough, Lee Chapman, Garry Parker

1989/90 League Cup Final
Nottingham Forest 1–0 Oldham Athletic

Nottingham Forest's second successive League Cup victory came at Oldham's expense, and equalled Liverpool's record of four wins in the competition at the time. Forest reached the final by beating Huddersfield Town, Crystal Palace, Everton, Tottenham and, in the semi-final, Coventry. Second Division Oldham Athletic weren't expected to beat highly-fancied Forest, but the Latics weren't going to lie down without a fight. However, despite Oldham's spirited first-half performance, Nigel Jemson scored for Forest early in the second half – and that's the way it stayed.

Forest's winning team: Steve Sutton; Brian Laws, Stuart Pearce; Des Walker, Steve Chettle, Steve Hodge; Gary Crosby, Garry Parker, Nigel Clough, Nigel Jemson, Franz Carr

1979/80 League Cup final
Wolverhampton Wanderers 1–0 Nottingham Forest

Reds fans must have thought this would be Forest's fifth League Cup victory having disposed of Liverpool in the semi-final, whereas Wolves had struggled to overcome Swindon Town. However, despite chucking everything but the kitchen sink at Wolves, Forest couldn't score. Then a stupid mix-up between Shilton and Needham allowed Andy Gray the simplest of tasks as he tapped the loose ball home for a 1–0 Wolves win.

Forest's runners-up team: Peter Shilton; Viv Anderson, Frank Gray; John McGovern, Dave Needham, Kenny Burns; Martin O'Neill, Ian Bowyer, Garry Birtles, Trevor Francis, John Robertson

1991/92 League Cup Final
Manchester United 1–0 Nottingham Forest
Forest beat Bolton, Bristol Rovers, Southampton, Crystal Palace and Tottenham to reach their sixth League Cup final (at this time known as the Rumbelows Cup). As with Forest's previous run of success in this competition in the 1970s, this was to end in defeat by a single goal scored by United's Brian McClair. Forest improved as the game went on, but were unable to get themselves back into the game.

Forest's runners-up team: Andy Marriott; Gary Charles (Brian Laws), Brett Williams; Des Walker, Darren Wassall, Roy Keane; Gary Crosby, Scot Gemmill, Nigel Clough, Teddy Sheringham, Kingsley Black

FOOTBALL'S ENGLISH HALL OF FAME

Nottingham Forest can be justifiably proud of having six men associated with the club inducted into the English Hall of Fame for their services to, or influence on, English football. They are: manager Brian Clough in 2002; players Peter Shilton in 2002, Viv Anderson and Roy Keane in 2004, Teddy Sheringham in 2009 and Stuart Pearce in 2010. In 2008 special awards were made by the European Hall of Fame honouring Brian Clough, Sir Matt Busby, Sir Alex Ferguson, Bob Paisley and Sir Bobby Robson (surely Clough and Paisley should receive posthumous knighthoods!).

FIRE!

On 24 August 1968 the Main Stand at the City Ground, which had been rebuilt in 1965, caught fire during the home game against Leeds United. The game, attended by 31,126 fans, was abandoned at half time – fortunately there were no casualties. Sadly the club lost many of its records, trophies and memorabilia as the largely wooden structure was reduced to a blackened shell. It was thought that the fire started in the dressing room area just prior to half time. Forest were forced to play their next six 'home' games at Meadow Lane – they didn't win any of them.

FIRST LEAGUE SEASON – 1892/93

Nottingham Forest finally joined the Football League in 1892, having won the Alliance the season before. They finished 10th out of 16 teams having taken 28 points from 30 games.

FIRST FOOTBALL LEAGUE GAME

This took place on 3 September 1892, in Division One against Everton away. The result was a 2–2 draw.
Forest's team that historic day: Brown; Earp, Scott; Hamilton, A. Smith, McCracken; McCallum, W. Smith, Higgins, Pike, McIness. Both Forest goals were scored by Pike.

FLOODLIGHTS

Nottingham Forest's first floodlit game at the City Ground was a League Cup tie against Gillingham, played on 11 September 1961. The attendance was 11,336. The concept of floodlighting events has been around since the seventeenth century, although in those far-off days the method was crude and not very practical. One hundred years later gas lamps were first used, then in 1874 the first electric light was patented, and things began to escalate. Again Nottingham Forest were at the forefront of an attempt to innovate. Following the Football Association's 1885 decision to allow clubs to use professional players in the FA Cup, there was an increasing need to generate more and more revenue from gate receipts to pay clubs' increasing wage bills. Forest and a number of other clubs had been experimenting with the notion of floodlights, each trying to safely light up games when it grew too gloomy to see clearly.

In March 1889 Forest played a game at their Gregory Ground in Lenton, lit by Wells lights. Wells lights used a high-power jet of oil to produce a flare of light equal to 2,000 candlepower. However, football fans would have to wait another 70-odd years because in 1888 the Football League banned the staging of floodlit football games. And in any case, Wells lighting was thought to be dangerous, and so it proved to be when in 1901 a stand at Swinton rugby ground was burned down after a Wells light had malfunctioned.

It wasn't until February 1956 that the first league game in England was played under floodlights when Newcastle beat Portsmouth 2–0 at Fratton Park. However, many floodlit friendly games had taken place prior to that.

FOOTBALL ALLIANCE

The Football Alliance was a short-lived rival to the Football League which had begun in 1988/89. The Alliance was formed by twelve clubs, one of which was Nottingham Forest, in time for the 1889/90 season. The Alliance lasted only three seasons, ceasing to exist after the 1891/92 campaign. Teams in the Football Alliance came from an area stretching from the Midlands to the North-East, including Grimsby,

Sheffield and Sunderland. The president of first champions The Wednesday, John Holmes, also became president of the Alliance. Champions in the second season were Stoke who had dropped out of the Football League after only two seasons (on both occasions the wooden spoonists). They stayed in the Alliance for just one season, winning the title, then for the following season Stoke, together with another Alliance club, Darwen, were accepted back into the Football League, taking its membership to fourteen clubs. Ardwick joined the Alliance in 1891 along with Burton Swifts and Lincoln City. The champions of the Football Alliance that season, 1891/92, were Nottingham Forest.

Prior to the 1892/93 season, the Football Alliance merged with the Football League, resulting in the formation of the Football League Second Division. The majority of the twelve clubs in the first season of this new division were drawn from the Football Alliance, although the three strongest Alliance clubs at that time – Nottingham Forest, The Wednesday and Newton Heath – joined the Football League First Division.

Football Alliance twelve original member clubs

Birmingham St Georges	Newton Heath
Bootle	Nottingham Forest
Crewe Alexandra	Small Heath
Darwen	Sunderland Albion
Grimsby Town	The Wednesday
Long Eaton Rangers	Walsall Town Swifts

Football Alliance champions

1889/90	The Wednesday
1890/91	Stoke
1891/92	Nottingham Forest

CLOUGHIE ON
FOOTBALL THINGS FOREIGN

'I bet their dressing room will smell of garlic rather than liniment over the next few months.'

Cloughie's view on the number of French players at Arsenal

'I can't even spell spaghetti never mind talk Italian. How could I tell an Italian to get the ball? He might grab mine.'

Cloughie's comment on the influx of foreign players in England

FOOTBALL LEAGUE CENTENARY
TOURNAMENT/
MERCANTILE CREDIT FESTIVAL CUP

In 1988, to commemorate and celebrate the 100th anniversary of the founding of the Football League, a Centenary Tournament was held, sponsored by Mercantile Credit. This 'festival' of football was staged on 16 and 17 April at Wembley Stadium. The following teams qualified to play in the tournament: Aston Villa, Blackburn Rovers, Crystal Palace, Everton, Leeds United, Liverpool, Luton Town, Manchester United, Newcastle United, Nottingham Forest, Sheffield Wednesday, Sunderland, Tranmere Rovers, Wigan Athletic, Wimbledon and Wolverhampton Wanderers – bizarrely, none of the big London clubs qualified. Qualification was via a set of criteria based upon that season's performance over a specific number of games.

Unfortunately for the League, apart from the first day of the tournament, attendances were very low with Wembley Stadium being less than a quarter full. Nine of the fifteen games played ended in draws and were won on penalties. Matches in the opening round were played over 40 minutes, not the normal 90 minutes, and it was due to this that a lot of games finished goalless, requiring sudden-death penalty shoot-outs to decide the winner.

The Football League Centenary Tournament final was contested by Nottingham Forest and Sheffield Wednesday. Eventually Forest won on penalties, having beaten Leeds United 3–0 in the opening round, Aston Villa in the quarter-final in a penalty shoot-out after a 0–0 draw, while Tranmere Rovers gave Forest a scare in the semis, drawing 2–2, with the Reds winning the penalty shoot-out.

The Football League marked the centenary with loads of events during the second half of 1987 and into 1988, including a Football League XI versus a Rest of the World XI match featuring that well known handler of the ball, Diego Maradona. League Champions Everton played Bayern Munich in a spicy mid-season game (remember that English clubs had been banned from playing in European competitions at that time). And the tournament sponsors put up another competition, the Mercantile Credit Centenary Trophy, which saw Arsenal beat Manchester United in the final (Forest had lost 4–1 in the quarter-final to Liverpool).

FOREST FIRSTS

Throughout their early years Forest were involved in some important pioneering developments in the game of football. At the Forest Recreation Ground shin-pads were used for the first time in 1874 when footballer and cricketer Sam Widdowson cut down a pair of cricket pads and strapped them to the outside of his socks to protect his shins from the then common practice of 'hacking' (see Sam Weller Widdowson, p. 127).

In 1878 Forest are credited as playing the first football game in which a whistle was used by a football umpire/referee – in those days an umpire patrolled each half of the pitch, shouting and waving a handkerchief to signal an infringement of the rules. The referee stood or sat on the touchline to keep time and mediate if the two umpires disagreed over a verdict. The game was versus Sheffield in the FA Cup second round on Saturday 21 December 1878, Forest winning 2–0.

At Forest's Town Ground, on 12 January 1891 (after earlier trials in Liverpool), nets were used in both goals for the first time. This was for a North v South representative match, watched by a Monday afternoon crowd of 4,000 and all the sport's leading officials, and refereed by Sam Widdowson. The nets had been designed by J.A. Brodie, the City Engineer of Liverpool, patented in 1891, and were described as 'a huge pocket into which the ball goes when a goal is scored.' Fred Geary of Everton (who was Nottingham-born) had the honour of testing them first, but although the nets were clearly an aid to referees, it took another 13 months for the FA to finally sanction their use – nothing changes.

In 1920 Nottingham Forest introduced the first elliptical-shaped goal posts – prior to that the shape of goalposts and crossbars were either round or square.

CLUB LEGEND – FRANK CLARK

Frank Albert Clark was born in Highfield, Geordieland, on 9 September 1943, playing for Crook Town before joining his local club Newcastle United, where he helped win the forerunner of the UEFA Cup, the Inter-Cities Fairs Cup, in 1969.

After 389 league appearances for the Magpies, Brian Clough signed him on a free transfer in February 1975, and he made his debut against Plymouth Argyle on 16 August 1975, going on to make 155 first-team appearances in a Forest shirt, and scoring one goal. He was an ever-present in the 1975/76 and 1976/77 season. Frank Clark will always be fondly

remembered as part of Cloughie's 1977/78 Championship-
and 1978/79 European Cup-winning team.

After being released by Forest in May 1981, he accepted
the position of assistant manager of Sunderland, and
subsequently became manager of Leyton Orient (after
serving as assistant manager), guiding them to promotion
via the 1989 Fourth Division play-offs. Two years later,
Clark was promoted to Managing Director, with Peter
Eustace taking over the managerial role. In May 1993, Frank
Clark followed the legendary Brian Clough as manager of
Nottingham Forest following Cloughie's retirement. Forest
had been relegated to Division One at the end of the 1992/93
season, but in reality Cloughie's team had been too good to
go down. Frank Clark took that team back to the Premier
League, as new Division One runners-up in 1993/94. The
following season, 1994/95, Clark led Forest to a third-place
finish in the Premier League, and in doing so qualified for
the 1995/96 UEFA Cup, where they knocked out Malmö,
Auxerre and Lyon before losing 7–2 in a superb showing
by Bayern Munich, inspired by three goals from Jurgen
Klinsmann in the semi-finals. Frank Clark's Forest finished
ninth in the Premier League in 1995/96.

In July 1993 Clark had signed Southend United's Stan
Collymore for £2.25 million; then sold him to Liverpool in
June 1995 for a record fee of £8.5 million.

Suddenly Frank Clark's luck ran out, and with Forest
heading for relegation, he resigned in December 1996. He
was back managing almost immediately with new Division
One club Manchester City, but after 15 months Clark was
sacked from his final management role with City heading for
relegation to the new Division Two.

Frank Clark is now the vice chariman of the League
Managers' Association.

FOUNDER MEMBERS OF THE CLUB

The 1865 committee:
A. Barks, W. Brown, W.P. Brown, C.F. Daft, T. Gamble, R.P. Hawksley, T.G. Howitt, W.L. Hussey, W.R. Lymberry, S. Milford, J.H. Rastall, W.H. Revis, J.G. Richardson, J.S. Scrimshaw and J. Tomlinson.

FOREST LEGENDS – FRED BEARDSLEY & A.J. BATES

In 1885 two Forest Football Club regulars, F.W. Beardsley and A.J. Bates, left Nottingham behind to find work in the nation's capital. These two enthusiastic footballers got jobs at the Woolwich Arsenal Armament Factory, and there being no local football team to play for, in 1886 they decided to help their co-workers form a team. The factory was located in an area called Dial Square, and had a sundial above the factory entrance, and so 'Dial Square Football Club' was the name they chose for their new team.

The name 'Dial Square' was soon changed to the much grander 'Royal Arsenal'. When, in 1891, the club turned professional, the team's name was changed to Woolwich Arsenal – subsequently being shortened to The Arsenal. Arsenal's first competitive match was set to be played on Plumstead Common in 1886, and legend has it that with the team having no worthwhile kit to wear for the game, Messrs Beardsley and Bates wrote to their old friends at Forest asking for their help. Forest responded by sending an entire red and white team strip plus a ball – hence the reason why Arsenal now play in red and white. Forest's sporting gesture was repaid in Forest's centenary year, when Arsenal presented Nottingham Forest with a silk team strip.

FULL MEMBERS' CUP

Following the Heysel Stadium disaster in 1985 and the subsequent banning of English football clubs from European competitions for five years, there was a need for a new cup competition to fill the vacuum, particularly to make up the revenue lost from those lucrative European games. The answer was a domestic cup competition imaginatively christened the Full Members' Cup, open to teams from Divisions One and Two. The model for the format was the Associate Members' Cup, which had been launched in 1984/85, open to clubs from Divisions Three and Four; a competition that had metamorphosed over time into the LDV Vans Trophy.

The Full Members' Cup competition ran for seven seasons starting in the 1985/86 season, and ending in 1991/92, never hitting the heights of popularity the league chairmen had dreamed about. Sponsorship for this competition proved to be hard to come by, but in 1988/89 a company called Simod came to the rescue. Simod withdrew their support after the 1989/90 competition, however, and the cudgel was taken up by Zenith Data Systems, who remained sponsors for three seasons until the tournament ceased to exist in 1990/91. Strangely, Arsenal, Liverpool, Manchester United and Tottenham declined to enter. Everton entered on three occasions and twice lost in the final. Twenty-one clubs entered the first competition which split teams into North and South pools, with regional semi-finals and finals, with the two regional winners fighting it out at Wembley Stadium. This structure was ditched after the first competition, and a knockout competition was adopted for three seasons. The regional format was brought back for the 1990/91 competition. Chelsea beat Manchester City 5–4 in the 1986 final, while two years later Reading beat Luton 4–1 in front of 61,740 fans. In 1989 Nottingham Forest edged out Everton in a seven-goal thriller after extra time and in 1992 won again, beating Southampton 3–2 after extra time. Chelsea lined up against Middlesbrough four years later with the teams being introduced before kick-off not to royalty or a football bureaucrat, but to a member of the ZDS staff – an admirably democratic gesture and perhaps the one innovation of the Full Members' Cup from which other competitions could learn.

The death knell came for this competition when English clubs were finally readmitted into Europe in time for the 1990/91 season. Zenith's sponsorship deal expired in 1992 and thus the competition evaporated into history.

1988/89 Simod Cup Final
Nottingham Forest 4–3 Everton, after extra time

Forest had already won the 1988/89 League Cup final, and now added the Simod Cup to their trophy cabinet with this thrilling victory at Wembley. Everton's Tony Cottee opened the scoring only to be pegged back when Garry Parker levelled from a corner – 1–1 at half time. Five minutes after the break Graeme Sharp restored Everton's lead. Once again Garry Parker came to Forest's rescue with a superb individual goal. The game went into extra time with Forest taking the lead for the first time in the match with a goal from Lee Chapman. Tony Cottee grabbed his second goal for Everton to make it 3–3. As full time approached, and the spectre of a penalty shoot-out loomed large, Forest substitute Franz Carr slung over a cross for Lee Chapman to toe-poke the winner past Neville Southall in the Everton goal.

Forest's winning team: Steve Sutton; Brian Laws, Stuart Pearce; Des Walker, Terry Wilson, Steve Hodge; Tommy Gaynor, Neil Webb, Nigel Clough, Lee Chapman, Garry Parker

1992 Zenith Data Systems Cup Final
Nottingham Forest 3–2 Southampton, after extra time

This was Forest's seventh visit to Wembley in four years, and it proved to be another happy one as Forest beat Southampton 3–2 with two goals from Scot Gemmill, plus one from Kingsley Black. Forest went two up before the Saints stormed back to force extra time, Scot Gemmill grabbing the winner;

his second of the game. This was to be the last trophy Brian Clough would win with Forest.

Forest: Andy Marriott; Gary Charles, Stuart Pearce; Des Walker, Darren Wassall, Roy Keane; Gary Crosby, Scot Gemmill, Nigel Clough, Teddy Sheringham, Kingsley Black

FOREST LEGEND – GARRY BIRTLES

Born in Nottingham on 27 July 1956, Garry arrived on the professional football scene like a meteor, transferring from non-league Long Eaton United to Forest in March 1977 for a reported fee of £30,000 and making his first-team debut against Hull City at the City Ground on 12 March. Following Peter Withe's transfer to Newcastle, Garry established himself in Forest's first team. In 1978/79, Garry banged in 26 goals in all competitions – 14 in the league, 6 in the League Cup including two in the winning final against Southampton (a game in which he also had 2 others disallowed) and of course 6 in the European Cup as he helped Forest to the crown of European Champions. In October 1980 Garry was transferred to Manchester United for a reported £1.25 million, scoring 11 goals in 57 appearances, plus 1 as substitute for the Red Devils, helping them to a third-place finish in 1980/81. He returned to the City Ground in September 1982 when Cloughie bought him back for around £275,000. After some time playing as a central defender, Birtles resumed his striking role in 1986/87 forging a strong partnership with the young Nigel Clough. In June 1987 Garry was given a free transfer and made the short journey across the Trent to join the Magpies, making the majority of his appearances at centre-half. From Meadow Lane he moved to Grimsby Town on a free in July 1989, staying until May 1992, and then joining Ilkeston Town in August 1992. Garry was assistant-manager to Paul Futcher at Gresley Rovers in 1993/94 before taking over as manager for the following season. Now pursuing a career in the media, having worked at Century 106 FM and Sky, he has also written for the *Nottingham Evening Post*. For Nottingham Forest Garry made a total of 278 appearances, 5 as substitute, scoring a total of 96 goals in all competitions. He also won 3 full England caps, to add to his 2 at under-21 level and 1 for England 'B.' In the 1978/79 season he was voted 'Young Player of the Year' by the Midland Sports Writers and was also 'Young European Footballer of the Year' in 1978.

GOALSCORERS

Top ten scorers of league goals:
199	Grenville Morris
123	Wally Ardron
119	Johnny Dent
105	Ian Storey-Moore
102	Nigel Clough
93	Enoch West
75	Tommy Wilson
70	Garry Birtles
69	Tommy Capel
68	Ian Bowyer

Top ten all-time scores of senior goals in all competitions:
217	Grenville Morris
131	Nigel Clough
124	Wally Ardron
122	Johnny Dent
118	Ian Storey-Moore
100	Enoch West
97	Ian Bowyer
96	Garry Birtles
95	John Robertson
90	Tommy Wilson

CLUB LEGEND –
GRENVILLE MORRIS

Forest's all-time top goalscorer, Welshman Arthur Grenville Morris, created a club record in 1902/03 by scoring in 8 consecutive League games for the club. Dave 'Boy' Martin equalled the run of games in 1936/37, but his total of 10 goals was one short of Morris. Grenville was born on 13 April 1877 in Builth Wells, Wales, briefly playing for his local team until moving to play for Aberystwyth Town, then for a short time at Bury and Swindon Town, before joining Forest in 1898. He made 457 appearances for the Reds, scoring 217 goals before retiring in 1913.

GROUNDS –
FOREST'S NOMADIC JOURNEY
TO THE CITY GROUND

Nottingham Forest's journey to the City Ground saw them call many places home, some briefly, some for much longer. The journey began at the Forest Recreation Ground in Nottingham (land that was once part of Sherwood Forest), also known as the Forest Racecourse (Nottingham Racecourse is now located at Colwick Park). This was the place where the club members first gathered to play a form of hockey called shinney. In 1865 the name of the venue also inspired the name the members chose to call their club: Forest Football Club. The venue consisted of a hippodrome-shaped racecourse (still retaining its shape today), and included a series of sports pitches in the centre. The site is still used to host the annual Nottingham Goose Fair.

In 1879 with the club wanting to establish a more appropriate home ground, the committee chose the Meadows, which was felt to be much more suitable to meet their growing ambitions. The Meadows was a piece of open ground situated on what is now named the Queen's Walk recreation ground (Queen's Walk having been named in honour of Queen Victoria's visit in 1843). Indeed, the Meadows had been the home ground of Notts County between 1864 and 1877 before they moved to Beeston Cricket Ground.

In 1879/80 Forest's success on the pitch, including reaching a second successive FA Cup semi-final, further fuelled the fires of ambition, and once again Forest were on the move after staying for only one season. Fortunately the best ground in Nottingham at that time was available for renting during the winter months – Trent Bridge Cricket Ground. Forest relocated there in 1880, but stayed only two seasons before once again moving on; this move was forced upon the club because they had been gazumped by Notts County who chose the cricket ground as their home venue (County's new paid secretary was also assistant secretary of Nottinghamshire County Cricket Club).

Reports indicate that Forest only realised they needed a new football ground just prior to the start of the new 1883/84 season, and so with most of the local pitches already taken, the club decided upon a pitch in Lenton as their new base. They named their new home Parkside, and it was sited at the north end of Derby Road, with entrances on Lenton Sands and Ilkeston Road. The exact location is not known. Apparently the local newspapers weren't too impressed with Forest's new ground compared with Trent Bridge – the pitch was uneven and sloped badly, and it was also quite a distance out of town. Making the ground suitable for staging football matches cost the club a few hundred pounds. However, in the end Forest were to stay at Parkside for three years. The first home fixture was a game against Small Heath Alliance (better known these days as Birmingham City). Forest won 3–2 watched by a sizeable crowd.

In 1884/85 Forest again won through to the semi-finals of the FA Cup, only to be beaten 3–0 in the replay by Queens Park from Scotland. The replay was played at Merchiston

Castle ground in Edinburgh, following a 1–1 draw in the first game.

Later in 1885 Forest relocated to yet another new home ground on Derby Road – Lenton United Cricket Club's ground at Gregory Ground, opposite Lenton recreation ground. Again they spent hundreds of pounds on levelling the pitch, erecting fencing, wooden stands holding 2,500 spectators (plus 500 seats reserved for club members) and moving the Parkside pavilion and dressing rooms. The new ground was ready for use by late September with the first home game taking place on 25 September 1885 when Forest beat Stoke 4–1. It was watched by a crowd in excess of 2,000. Fans and journalists alike appeared to like the new venue, and in November 1885, in atrocious weather, a few short of 10,000 people turned up to watch Notts County beat Forest 4–1. It was at this football ground that Forest first staged a floodlit match in March 1889, using Wells lights (see p. 68).

Unfortunately for Forest, football fans in Nottingham seemed to prefer matches closer to the town centre, namely Trent Bridge, where larger revenues were regularly being generated, and this seems to have been one of the factors taken into account when the Football League was formed in 1888, with Notts County chosen as one of the original twelve founder members (unsurprisingly the twelve clubs all fielded paid 'professional' players in their teams). In their infinite wisdom, the ruling body of the Football League were reluctant to include more than one team from a town or city, so Forest joined the newly formed Football Alliance for the 1889/90 season.

There was no doubt that football was becoming ever more popular. In Nottingham, County were regularly attracting crowds of over 3,000, compared to much lower numbers prepared to travel to Lenton to watch Forest. Something needed to be done. The answer was that at the club's AGM members voted overwhelmingly to become professional. However, the following 'professional' season did not have a sufficiently positive effect on the gate receipts. The committee decided that the club's development was not only being hampered by not enlisting top quality professional players, but also by not being close enough to the city centre to raise the revenue to pay these players.

Finally, in July 1890, a new ground was identified in the Trent Bridge area, a ground known as 'Councillor Woodward's Field', situated at the end of Arkwright Street. The ground was renamed the Town Ground, but needed a lot of costly work to bring it up to the required standard. Around £1,000 was spent on such things as levelling the pitch, building up the banking and erecting a stand. Unfortunately the new ground was not ready in time for the start of the 1890/91 season, so the team's early Football Alliance fixtures had to be played at Lenton.

On 'Goose Fair' Thursday 2 October 1890, Forest's Town Ground was officially opened by the Lord Mayor of Nottingham. The club had originally invited Football League founder members Wolverhampton Wanderers to inaugurate their new ground, but there was a problem with this. A clash of interests came into play when Notts County tendered a strong objection because they had scheduled a league game against Bolton Wanderers for the same afternoon. Against the threat of being banned from playing against future Football League opposition, Forest had no choice but to change their opponents for the inaugural game, inviting previous FA Cup semi-final opponents Queen's Park from Glasgow instead. Forest's match at the Town Ground was attended by around 3,500 fans, compared to the 6,000 or so who attended County's game. It was mentioned in the press that Arkwright Street was 'exceedingly thronged and there was a good deal of badinage indulged by the travelling supporters of each club.'

Fortunately County's protest didn't cause any lasting bad feeling and the two rival clubs remained on good terms. A good thing for Notts County, because when summer cricket took priority at the beginning and end of each season,

Nottingham Forest allowed County to play their home games at the Town Ground. In return, in 1892 Notts County supported Forest's application to join the Football League, with the stipulation that the Magpies were allocated home fixtures against the five best clubs in the league prior to those clubs playing Forest.

By the time Forest won their first FA Cup final in 1897/98, the decision to leave the Town Ground and move the club's home to a more spacious site in West Bridgford on the other side of the River Trent, had been made.

Grounds – Summary

Forest Recreation Ground	1865–79
The Meadows	1879–80
Trent Bridge	1880–82
Parkside, Lenton	1882–85
Gregory Ground, Lenton	1885–90
The Town Ground	1890–98
The City Ground, West Bridgford	1898–

CLUB LEGENDS

Harold S. Radford – Forest Secretary-Manager 1889 to 1897

Businessman Harry Radford was appointed secretary-manager in July 1889, having served as secretary from 1886 to 1888, guiding the club to the Football Alliance title in 1892 and the subsequent entry into the Football League the following season. Harry Radford also served on the FA Council.

Harry Hallam – Forest Secretary-Manager 1897 to 1909

Harry Hallam's claim to fame is leading the Reds to FA Cup glory in 1898.

HEAD TO HEADS

Forest's head-to-head meetings with their three main local rivals are always passionate affairs. Here is a summary:

Nottingham Forest versus Derby County
Forest versus the Rams in league games:
Home: Nottingham Forest 18 wins, 10 draws, Derby 11 wins
Goals: Forest 78, Rams 60.
Away: Nottingham Forest 14 wins, 9 draws, Derby 15 wins
Goals: Forest 48, Rams 60.

Forest versus the Rams in cup games
First the FA Cup. The two clubs have contested eight FA Cup games:
Nottingham Forest 3 wins (including the final in 1898),
Derby 5 wins, 2 games were drawn, both teams winning one of the replays.

In the League Cup the clubs have met just once:
Forest won 2–1 at Derby in round three on 30 October 1985.

The only other meeting was in the Anglo-Italian Cup:
Derby won this one 3–2 on 8 September 1993 at Derby.

Summary of head-to-heads with Derby County
Nottingham Forest 35 wins to Derby County's 31;
21 games ended in a draw.
Total goals scored: Forest 138, Derby 136

Nottingham Forest versus Leicester City
Forest versus the Foxes in league games:
Home: Forest 26 wins, 9 draws, Leicester 10 wins
Goals: Forest 87, Foxes 49.
Away: Forest 8 wins, 11 draws, Leicester 27 wins
Goals: Forest 55, Foxes 84.

Forest versus the Foxes in cup games
The two clubs have only ever met once in the FA Cup:
Nottingham Forest won 5–1 at home, round one, on
9 February 1901.

In the League Cup the clubs have met three times:
On 30 November 1988 in round four, at Leicester, a 0–0
draw, Nottingham Forest winning the replay 2–1.
They met again in round two on 18 September 2007,
Leicester beating Forest 3–2 in Nottingham.

The only other meetings were in the Zenith Data Systems
Cup:
Forest won 3–1 on aggregate. Having drawn 1–1 at Leicester
on 12 February 1992, Forest won their home leg 2–0 on
26 February 1992.

Summary of head-to-heads with Leicester City
Nottingham Forest: 37 wins to Leicester City's 38,
22 games ended in a draw.
Total goals scored: Forest 154, Leicester 139

Nottingham Forest versus Notts County
Forest versus the Magpies in league games:
Home: Forest 21 wins, 8 draws, Magpies 14 wins
Goals: Forest 56, Magpies 41
Away: Forest 14 wins, 15 draws, Magpies 14 wins
Goals: Forest 64, Magpies 66

Forest versus the Magpies in cup games
The two clubs have contested six FA Cup games, all in the
nineteenth century:
Nottingham Forest 3 wins; 1 draw, at Forest, Notts County
winning the replay 4–1 at home. Including this game County
have won 2 games.

In the League Cup the clubs have only met once:
On 25 October 1977 in round three, Forest won 4–0 at home.

The only other meetings were in the Anglo-Italian Cup, and
the Anglo-Scottish Cup, one game in each, where both games
ended in a draw:
Anglo-Italian Cup on 15 September 1993, 1–1 at Forest.
Anglo-Scottish Cup on 7 August 1976, 0–0 at County.

Summary of head-to-heads with Notts County
Nottingham Forest 39 wins to Notts County's 30,
26 games ended in a draw.
Total goals scored: Forest 136, County 118

OVERSEAS FOOTBALLERS

Many fine foreign footballers have played for Nottingham
Forest, here are a few:

Australia	David Tarka
Canada	Jim Brennan
Croatia	Nikola Jerkan
France	Thierry Bonalair, Mattieu Louis-John
Germany	Eugen Bopp
Ghana	Junior Agogo
Holland	Hans van Breukelen, Pierre van Hooijdonk, Bryan Roy, John Metgod
Iceland	Brynjar Gunnarsson, Toddy Orlygsson
Jamaica	David Johnson, Marlon King
Norway	Alf-Inge Haaland, Lars Bohinen, Einar Jan Aas, Kjetil Osvald, Jon Olav Hjelde
Poland	Radoslaw Majewski
Switzerland	Raimondo Pont, Marco Pasolo
Trinidad & Tobago	Stern John
USA	Robbie Findlay, Ben Olsen, John Harkes

THE HILLSBOROUGH DISASTER –
SATURDAY 15 APRIL 1989

This was a catastrophe waiting to happen. Security fences and penning, added to an inadequate method of ticketing, were all constituent parts of the problem – fans being treated like cattle to be herded with disdain by those with the power to do so. It wasn't as though it hadn't happened before. At the Hillsborough semi-final between Spurs and Wolves on 11 April 1981, 38 people were injured.

On that awful day, 15 April 1989, many factors conspired to complicate what happened – factors that taken in isolation possibly might not have caused a problem, but when combined created one of, if not the, blackest day in English football history. Ninety-six innocent football fans tragically died as a result of what happened on that dreadful day.

The police had allocated the Spion End of the stadium to Forest fans which held 21,000, whereas Liverpool fans were allocated the Leppings Lane End, with a capacity of 14,600. Considering the relative size of the average attendance of each club this would appear to have been an error. Unannounced road works on the M62 delayed Liverpool fans as they made their way across the Pennines, significantly adding to the mass of fans trying to get into the Leppings Lane End prior to kick-off. The turnstiles weren't able to cope fast enough, and so could not help ease the pressure that had and was still building up outside the ground. By 3 p.m. the estimate is that more than 5,000 Liverpool fans were still outside the stadium. Then the game kicked off at 3 p.m. These days it would be nice to think that the kick-off would have been delayed while the fans took their places. At this point, Brian Clough's own words are a poignant insight into the emotion of that day – 'We thought we were 90 minutes from Wembley. It turned out we were 5 minutes from hell,' in an extract taken from the chapter 'Death in the Afternoon' of *Clough – The Autobiography*.

The Taylor Report on this tragedy changed many things for football fans, but it was too late to save the lives of those who suffered the ultimate consequence just for going to watch their team play a football match. After 6 minutes, when finally the unfolding tragedy became apparent, referee Ray Lewis was advised by the police to halt the game, and the two teams left the pitch not to return that day. It was estimated that at least 700 people were injured, 20 seriously, but the death toll that day grew to 94, 2 more fans subsequently pssing away. At the inquest the coroner returned a verdict of accidental death. It is believed that many of those who died were still alive at 3.15 p.m., and perhaps, given proper medical assistance, might have survived. To this day families of the bereaved continue to campaign for the inquest to be reopened.

At Old Trafford on 7 May 1989 Forest lost the rescheduled FA Cup semi-final, beaten 3–1 by Liverpool.

CLOUGHIE ON PLAYERS AND MANAGERS

'Stand up straight, get your shoulders back and get your hair cut.'

Cloughie's words of advice at Hartlepool to the young John McGovern

'The ugliest player I ever signed was Kenny Burns.'

Cloughie's version of a complimentary comment about Kenny Burns

'Take your hands out of your pockets.'

Cloughie's advice to a young Trevor Francis as he received an award from Cloughie

'I only ever hit Roy the once. He got up so I couldn't have hit him very hard.'

Cloughie's famous remark about controlling Roy Keane

'He's learned more about football management than he ever imagined. Some people think you can take football boots off and put a suit on. You can't do that.'

Cloughie's view on David Platt's first season as manager of Nottingham Forest

'Anybody who can do anything in Leicester but make a jumper has got to be a genius.'

Doing his bit for East Midlands relations

'If he'd been English or Swedish, he'd have walked the England job.'

Cloughie's tributes to Martin O'Neill

'That Seaman is a handsome young man but he spends too much time looking in his mirror rather than at the ball. You can't keep goal with hair like that.'

Cloughie's comment on England and Arsenal's pony-tailed goalkeeper David Seaman

'The Derby players have seen more of his balls than the one they're meant to be playing with.'

Cloughie's view on the streaker at a Derby County game versus Manchester United

IN THE BEGINNING …
THE ORIGINS OF FOOTBALL
AND FOREST'S EARLY HISTORY

The origins of the game of football are in many ways shrouded in the mists of time, probably because few ancient clerics deigned football sufficiently important enough to devote quill and ink to the detailed recording of it. Wouldn't it be great if there were ancient accounts of matches between historical adversaries such as Picts Athletic versus Ancient

Britons United, or Julius Caesar's Roman Select XI versus Boudicca Academicals? Having said this, we do know that history indicates that some form of football using an air-filled ball seems to have been engaged in by the Ancient Greeks and the Romans, and before this in China well over 2,000 years ago, while the Japanese had their own version of footy; in fact the indigenous peoples of most continents appear to have kicked a ball about as a form of exercise to help strengthen legs and respiratory systems.

There are any number of references to football in medieval England that have made it through the centuries to provide us with some idea of how the game developed. It is quite possible that the Romans brought the game with them when they decided to give the Ancient Britons a good kicking (they really only wanted our tin!) when they nipped across the Channel in about 55 BC. Others have suggested that the Normans brought a version of football with them when they sailed over in 1066 to give us another good kicking.

Whoever it was, by the Middle Ages popular Shrove Tuesday games of 'mob football' were on the rise. An account was written in the late twelfth century describing youthful activities in London involving kicking a ball about, and in 1280 some chap playing football in the North-East apparently ran into the dagger of an opponent (that's got to hurt!). Then in 1308 a football spectator in Newcastle was charged with stabbing a player. Many more records of violence are in existence, making our modern game sound like a game for 'Jessies'.

At various times football was deemed so violent that it was banned by some of our merry monarchs. Kings Edward II and Edward III had a go (penalties probably weren't a shot at goal, but involved a confiscation of one's ball, or balls!); in Ed the Third's case, he wanted no distractions to get in the way of archery practice. However, football obviously didn't go away because King Henry IV introduced a levy on playing the game.

Two of our most famous writers mention football in their works: Geoffrey Chaucer includes a tenuous reference in 'The Knight's Tale' in his *Canterbury Tales*. After the knight has been unhorsed, 'He rolleth under foot as doth a ball.' A bit later, William Shakespeare mentions the game in *King Lear* and in *The Comedy of Errors*.

An activity described as a 'kicking game' with marked-out boundaries was recorded as being played in the late fifteenth century at Cawston in Nottinghamshire – maybe Nottingham invented the football pitch? However, not all monarchs were against the game, King James I actually encouraged Christians to play football after Sunday worship.

By the mid-nineteenth century football was being played by 'Gentlemen's Clubs' and in a large number of public schools, where the game was first organised into a set of codes, including a form of the offside rule; although this seems to have varied from school to school. The game had been adopted by the gentry and by the public school system because it promoted competitiveness and fitness. Pupils at these schools had the free time to devote their energies to codifying the game, unlike the 'unwashed masses' who worked at least six days a week, mostly twelve hours or more a day – these workers had no time or energy to play sport. However, the Factory Act of 1850 was to change this emphasis by introducing restrictions to the working hours, in particular the ceasing of work at 2 p.m. on Saturdays. The resultant 'free' Saturday afternoon, coupled with the earlier explosion of rail travel, now gave rise to the popularity of outings and sport.

Another major factor in the development of sport was the invention and patenting of the lawnmower in 1830 thus greatly improving the surface on which football and other sports could be played.

Various footballing 'Gymnastic Societies' had sprung up in the country in the late eighteenth and early nineteenth centuries; there are records of one such club in Edinburgh where football was played between 1824 and 1841, and some may lay claim to be the oldest 'football club' still in existence. However, the form of the game played there is not clearly recorded; it seems likely that some clubs played rugby.

Football continued to grow in popularity as the nineteenth century progressed, although the rules governing the games were different and varied. The 'Cambridge Rules' of 1848 appear to have been the first, followed by the 'Sheffield FC Rules' in 1855, and then another 'Cambridge Rules' put together at Cambridge University by John Charles Thring and Henry de Winton in 1862. Then, in 1863, when Ebenezer Cobb Morley proposed the creation of the Football Association, these three sets of rules were combined into one, although some more recalcitrant clubs declined to change from the Sheffield Rules until 1878.

Over the course of the next few years the rules of the game developed, and when the FA Cup competition was introduced in 1871 all matches were played under one set of rules. Clubs were still amateur – professionalism was banned – so the competition was dominated by teams from the armed services or teams of old boys from public schools. A number of clubs were accused of employing professional players and in 1885 the FA legalised the use of professionals.

Nottingham Forest Football and Bandy Club officially came into being in 1867, although two years earlier in 1865 the first team was formed, playing their first match on 22 March 1866 against Notts County Football Club who had been founded three years earlier in 1862. In 1865 with the game of football growing in popularity in Nottingham and the country as a whole, a group of men, players of the popular game of 'shinney' (a game similar to hockey) held a special meeting in the Clinton Arms on Shakespeare Street, Nottingham, where a man by the name of J.S. Scrimshaw successfully proposed a switch of games from 'shinney' to football. Bandy was a game similar to shinney, but played in the winter. At the special meeting, the committee also passed a resolution to purchase a dozen red caps with tassels, announcing that the team colours should be 'Garibaldi Red'. This decision was made in honour of Giuseppe Garibaldi, the Italian patriot who was the leader of the popular Italian freedom fighters known as the 'Red Shirts Party'. Forest have worn red since that day.

In those days football clubs identified themselves as much by their headgear as the colour of their shirts. Forest were the first football club to 'officially' wear red shirts and caps, a colour since adopted by many others clubs. Following the acceptance of Scrimshaw's proposals, and the team's first official football match, there followed a brief transitional period, during which time a new committee was established, and the playing of shinney was dropped altogether in favour of football – 'Nottingham Forest Football Club' was born.

In the 1878/79 season Forest's team was greatly strengthened when the Notts Castle Club was disbanded and decided to join Forest; the influx of additional talent helped form Forest into a powerful team. Forest decided to enter the 1878 FA Challenge Cup competition for the first time, following Notts County's entry into the previous year's competition. Ironically the two Nottingham teams were drawn to play each other in the first round. The match was played at the Beeston cricket ground, Forest winning 3–1.

That season Forest reached their first semi-final.

HONOURS

A chronological roll of honour:

Football Alliance champions	1891/92
FA Cup winners	1898
Division Two champions	1906/07
Victory Shield champions	1918/19
Division Two champions	1921/22
Division Three South champions	1950/51
Division Two runners-up	1956/57
FA Cup winners	1959
FA Charity Shield runners-up	1959
Division One runners-up	1966/67
Anglo-Scottish Cup winners	1976/77
Division One champions	1977/78
FA Charity Shield winners	1978
League Cup winners	1977/78
European Cup winners	1978/79
League Cup winners	1978/79
Division One runners-up	1978/79
European Cup winners	1979/80
European Super Cup winners	1979/80
League Cup runners-up	1980
Nuremberg Tournament winners	1982
Trofeo Colombino Cup winners	1982
Mercantile Credit Festival Cup winners	1988
League Cup winners	1988/89
Simod/Zenith Data Systems Cup winners	1988/89
League Cup winners	1989/90
FA Cup runners-up	1991
Simod/Zenith Data Systems Cup winners	1992
League Cup runners-up	1992
Division One runners-up	1993/94
Division One champions	1997/98
League One runners-up	2007/08

FOREST LEGEND – IAN BOWYER

'Mr Versatile' was born in Ellesmere Port on 6 June 1951, birthplace of two other footballing giants in Stan Cullis and Joe Mercer. Bowyer had originally made his name at Manchester City, but he was at Leyton Orient when Dave MacKay bought him for Forest in October 1973. He went on to make a total of 541 appearances, plus 23 as substitute (the second all-time highest number of appearances for Nottingham Forest), in two spells with the club, scoring many vital goals among his very respectable total of 96 (joint seventh alongside Garry Birtles in Forest's top ten all-time goal-scorers). He was sold to Sunderland in January 1981, but Clough bought him back in January 1982, before eventually releasing him in May 1987.

FOREST LEGEND – IAN STOREY-MOORE

Fans' favourite and winger Ian was born in Ipswich on 17 January 1945, joining Forest as an amateur in 1961, turning professional in May 1962. He went on to make 271+1 appearances for the Reds, scoring 118 goals.

In 1972 Cloughie famously paraded Moore at the Baseball Ground as his new signing, when in fact he hadn't signed for Derby. The Rams received a severe reprimand from the FA and were fined £5,000 for this indiscretion. Several weeks later Ian joined Manchester United for around £200,000. Sadly he was forced to retire from football on medical grounds in December 1973 having made 39 appearances for United, scoring 11 goals. He moved on to Chicago Sting, then as player-manager at Shepshed Charterhouse and Burton Albion. His most recent role in football was as chief scout at Aston Villa under Martin O'Neill.

THE NOTTINGHAM FOREST MISCELLANY

INTERCONTINENTAL CUP

Nottingham Forest were runners-up in the 1980/81 competition, beaten 1–0 by Nacional of Uruguay in Tokyo's National Stadium on 11 February 1981; the first time the match had been staged on neutral territory. The Intercontinental Cup, sometimes called the European/South American Cup, was set up to be a World Club Championship, supported by UEFA and their South American counterpart, CONMEBOL, and played by the European Cup holders and the holders of the Copa Libertadores, the South American equivalent. The inaugural match was in 1960, between Real Madrid and Penarol of Uruguay.

FOREST LEGEND – JACK BURKITT

Nottingham Forest legend John 'Jack' Orgill Burkitt was born in Wednesbury on 19 January 1926, made 503 senior appearances for the Reds, and scored 12 goals. He joined Forest from Darlaston Town in May 1947, earning a regular first-team place at left-half. As captain he led the Reds to cup final glory in 1959, having helped Forest to two promotions, including the Third Division South championship. After his playing career finished he remained at the club as one of the coaching staff, before becoming manager of Notts County in 1966. The following year he joined Derby County as trainer under Brian Clough, although he left them owing to ill heath in 1969. He died on 12 September 2003 in Brighouse.

BRIAN CLOUGH, MP?

Brian Clough was a life-long socialist and supporter of the Labour Party – indeed, Labour twice tried to persuade Cloughie to accept a nomination as a parliamentary candidate. Despite Cloughie's refusal he did, however, agree to campaign for Derby MP Phillip Whitehead. Clough's favourite politician, Michael Foot, is reported to have said of him, 'He always had a strong political sense and a keen understanding of socialist principles . . . The rank and file Labour supporter loves him. He is one of them. If people would only listen to him more carefully, they'd deal with hooliganism much better than they do.'

CLOUGHIE ON CHEATS

'It was a crooked match and he was a crooked referee. That was a tournament we could and should have won.'
Cloughie's scathing comments after Forest had lost the 1984 UEFA Cup semi-final to Anderlecht

'No cheating bastards will I talk to; I will not talk to any cheating bastards!'
Cloughie's refusal to speak to anyone associated with Anderlecht

FOREST LEGEND – JOHN MCGOVERN

Born in Montrose on 28 October 1949, Cloughie's captain John Prescott McGovern was undoubtedly a favourite of Brian Clough, playing for him at Hartlepool, Derby and Leeds, arriving at Forest from Leeds United in February 1975 shortly after the great man. He went on to make 253 league appearances for Forest, scoring 6 goals. John left Forest for

Bolton Wanderers in June 1982 as player-manager until January 1985, hanging up his playing boots in 1984. He later managed Horwich RMI from 1985 to 1986, then moved to Tenerife before returning as manager of Chorley in February 1990. Next came a spell as assistant manager to Peter Shilton at Plymouth Argyle from March 1992 until September 1994 when he took the job as joint manager of Rotherham United with Archie Gemmill – this only lasted until September 1996. John was manager of Woking from 1997 to 1998, and had a spell with Ilkeston Town, before becoming an after-dinner speaker, and working as a summariser for BBC Radio Nottingham alongside Colin Fray.

KOP THAT

On 27 September 1978, in the first round, second leg tie of the 1979/80 European Cup, plucky Nottingham Forest memorably silenced the Kop at Anfield by drawing 0–0 on the night, winning the tie 2–0 on aggregate. They had beaten Liverpool 2–0 in the first leg at the City Ground on 13 September 1978.

FOREST LEGEND – JOHNNY DENT

Centre-forward John George Dent was born in Spennymoor on 31 January 1903. He played for Spennymoor Rangers, Tudhoe United, Durham City, Tow Law Town and Huddersfield Town before arriving at Nottingham Forest in October 1929. He went on to score 122 goals including 4 league hat-tricks, plus 1 in the FA Cup, across 207 appearances. In 1937 he moved to Kidderminster Harriers, where he played until May 1939. He served in the RAF during the Second World War, going on to play cricket for West Bridgford CC. Johnny Dent died on 6 November 1979 in West Bridgford.

FOREST LEGEND – JOHN ROBERTSON

Left winger John Robertson (a genius of a footballer) was born in Uddingston near Glasgow on 20 January 1953, joining Forest as an apprentice in May 1970. Robbo went on to make 499 appearances for the Reds, plus 15 as substitute, scoring 95 goals. His deceptive looks masked the propensity for incredible bursts of speed over short distances, a good attribute for any footballer, but as a winger, it gave him the edge over defenders. Who could forget the inch-perfect cross to the head of Trevor Francis which won the European Cup for Forest in the Olympic Stadium, Munich, on 30 May 1979, beating Malmö 1–0? A year later Robbo scored the vital goal against Kevin Keegan's highly fancied Hamburg to retain that coveted trophy. In June 1983, the by then manager of Derby, Peter Taylor, snatched him away from Cloughie's grasp for a spell at the Baseball Ground before Robbo returned to Forest in August 1985. John won 28 caps for Scotland, scoring 8 goals, playing for the ill-fated Ally MacLeod's Scotland in one of their three games in the 1978 World Cup finals in Argentina (the disappointing 1–1 draw with Iran). In recent times he has been assistant manager to Martin O'Neill at Celtic and Aston Villa.

LEAGUE RUNNERS-UP

Nottingham Forest have been runners-up in their league on five occasions:

First Division	1966/67 & 1978/79
Second Division	1956/57 & 1993/94 (Division One)
Third Division	2007/08 (League One)

FOREST LEGEND –
JIMMY GORDON (TRAINER)

Another from Cloughie's time at Middlesbrough, Jimmy Gordon was one of the older fraternity of Boro' players, which is where he first met Brian Clough and Peter Taylor. He first made his name in football before the Second World War with Newcastle United, and then at Middlesbrough after the hostilities ended, where he made 231 league appearances, scoring 3 goals between 1946 and 1953. He coached at Derby County before Clough and Taylor persuaded him to join them at Nottingham Forest. Jimmy Gordon sadly died in 1996.

FOREST LEGEND – KENNY BURNS

Brian Clough gave Kenny the night off from the final league game of the 1977/78 season to allow him to pick up his Footballer of the Year award at the soccer writers' dinner in London. The one-time bad-boy, striker-cum-defender of Birmingham City, now reformed Nottingham Forest central defender, thoroughly deserved his accolade. Clough had seen the talent and the temperament of Kenny Burns, already capped by Scotland at centre-forward, and had decided he was the man for him. He got his man for a measly £150,000. Most football pundits thought him mad, even at that price, but as usual, Clough ignored them, confident he could turn this Scot into a world-class defender.

And he was right. Burns was selected for Scotland's World Cup squad as a central defender at the end of his first full season playing in defence. Born in Glasgow on 23 September 1953, the Scottish international was a solid defender, hard but skilful. His reputation of being short on discipline was reversed at the City Ground – he was only booked once in Forest's League Championship-winning season, and that was for time-wasting.

He went on to win 20 caps for his country, scoring 1 goal, to go with all his other achievements. In a fairly short career with Forest, Kenny Burns made 137 league appearances, scoring 13 goals. He was transferred to Leeds United in October 1981, before subsequently joining Derby County.

FOREST LEGEND – LARRY LLOYD

A stalwart of Forest's defence, centre-back Laurence Valentine 'Larry' Lloyd joined Forest from Coventry City (for whom he made 50 appearances, scoring 5 goals) in October 1976, a bargain buy for a reported £60,000 fee, initially as an on-loan signing. Larry took over Sammy Chapman's role at the heart of the Reds' defence. Born in Bristol on 6 October 1948, Lloyd began his playing career at Bristol Rovers, making 43 appearances and scoring 1 goal. Big Larry became a firm favourite with the Forest fans with his no-nonsense style of play, going on to make 148 league appearances for the Reds, scoring 6 goals. He had originally made his name with the other Reds, Liverpool, playing for them in their losing FA Cup final against Arsenal in 1971. He didn't make Liverpool's final eleven for 1974 Cup final, when they beat Newcastle 3–0, but was an ever-present in Liverpool's 1972/73 Championship-winning side, also helping them to win the UEFA Cup in 1972/73. He made 150 appearances for the Anfield side, scoring 4 goals. Larry also won 4 full England caps.

Lloyd was sold from Forest to Wigan Athletic in March 1981, where he became player-manager. From there, in 1983, he moved to First Division Notts County, taking over the manager's role from Jimmy Sirrel. Larry left following County's relegation to Division Two at the end of the 1983/84 season and eventually embarked on a radio career as a football pundit with GEM AM, and with Century 106, later moving to Spain where he became manager of amateur club Real Marbella.

THE GAFFERS

Harry Radford	1889–97
Harry Hallam	1897–1909
Fred Earp	1909–12
Bob Marsters	1912–25
John Baynes	1925–29
Stan Hardy	1930–31
Noel Watson	1931–36
Harold Wightman	1936–39
Billy Walker	1939–60
Andy Beattie	1960–63
Johnny Carey	1963–68
Matt Gillies	1969–72
Dave Mackay	1972–73
Allan Brown	1973–75
Brian Clough	1975–93
Frank Clark	1993–96
Stuart Pearce*	1996–97
Dave Bassett	1997–98
Micky Adams*	1999 (January)
Ron Atkinson	1999 (4 months)
David Platt	1999–2001
Paul Hart	2001–04
Joe Kinnear	2004
Mick Harford*	2004–05
Gary Megson	2005–February 2006
Frank Barlow* & Ian McParland*	February–May 2006
Colin Calderwood	2006–December 2008
John Pemberton*	2008
Billy Davies	Jan 2009–June 2011
Steve McClaren	June 2011–

* Denotes caretaker manager

FOREST LEGEND – MARTIN O'NEILL

Born in Kilrea, Northern Ireland, on 1 March 1952, Martin O'Neill was signed by Forest in October 1971, and had 10 seasons at the City Ground. Without doubt, in his heyday he was one of the finest right-sided midfield players around. He made 264 league appearances for Forest, plus 21 as substitute, scoring 48 goals. Martin won 39 caps for Northern Ireland. He transferred to Norwich for a fee of £250,000 in February 1981, where he made only 11 league appearances, before moving to Manchester City, and 12 league games later, back to Norwich, and then to Notts County. He went on to manage Wycombe Wanderers and Leicester City prior to landing the plum job of manager of Celtic. His next job was as manager of Aston Villa, with Robbo as his assistant. O'Neill shocked the football world in 2010 by walking away from the Villa job.

NORTHERN IRELAND INTERNATIONALS

The most notable international footballing Ulstermen who played for Nottingham Forest are:

Martin O'Neill	64 caps
Tommy Wright	35 caps
Gary Fleming	31 caps
Tommy Wright (the goalkeeper)	31 caps
Kingsley Black	30 caps
Sammy Clingan	25 caps
Alan Fettis	25 caps
Liam O'Kane	20 caps
David Campbell	10 caps

Not all caps were won while at Nottingham Forest.

CLOUGHIE ON FOOTBALL

'If God had wanted us to play football in the clouds, he'd have put grass up there.'

Cloughie on the importance of passing to feet and playing football on the deck

'You don't want roast beef and Yorkshire pudding every night and twice on Sunday.'

Cloughie's view about too much football on television

'Football hooligans? Well there are ninety-two club chairmen for a start.'

Cloughie on hooligans

'If a player had said to Bill Shankly, "I've got to speak to my agent," Bill would have hit him. And I would have held him while he hit him.'

Cloughie on agents

'I like my women to be feminine, not sliding into tackles and covered in mud.'

Cloughie's controversial views on women's football

NOTTINGHAM FOREST'S COMPLETE, SEASON-BY-SEASON FOOTBALL LEAGUE RECORD

Season	Competition	Position
1878/79	FA Cup only	–
1879/80	FA Cup only	–
1880/81	FA Cup only	–
1881/82	FA Cup only	–

Season	Competition	Position
1882/83	FA Cup only	–
1883/84	FA Cup only	–
1884/85	FA Cup only	–
1885/86	FA Cup only	–
1886/87	FA Cup only	–
1887/88	FA Cup only	–
1888/89	FA Cup only	–
1889/90	Football Alliance	–
1890/91	Football Alliance	–
1891/92	Football Alliance	1st (champions)
1892/93	Division One	10th
1893/94	Division One	7th
1894/95	Division One	7th
1895/96	Division One	13th
1896/97	Division One	11th
1897/98	Division One	8th
1898/99	Division One	11th
1899/1900	Division One	8th
1900/01	Division One	4th
1901/02	Division One	5th
1902/03	Division One	10th
1903/04	Division One	9th
1904/05	Division One	16th
1905/06	Division One	19th (relegated)
1906/07	Division Two	1st (champions)
1907/08	Division One	9th
1908/09	Division One	14th
1909/10	Division One	14th
1910/11	Division One	20th (relegated)
1911/12	Division Two	15th
1912/13	Division Two	17th
1913/14	Division Two	20th
1914/15	Division Two	18th

SUSPENDED OWING TO FIRST WORLD WAR

1919/20	Division Two	18th

Season	Competition	Position
1920/21	Division Two	18th
1921/22	Division Two	1st (champions)
1922/23	Division One	20th
1923/24	Division One	20th
1924/25	Division One	22nd (relegated)
1925/26	Division Two	17th
1926/27	Division Two	5th
1927/28	Division Two	10th
1928/29	Division Two	11th
1929/30	Division Two	10th
1930/31	Division Two	17th
1931/32	Division Two	11th
1932/33	Division Two	5th
1933/34	Division Two	17th
1934/35	Division Two	9th
1935/36	Division Two	19th
1936/37	Division Two	18th
1937/38	Division Two	20th
1938/39	Division Two	20th
SUSPENDED OWING TO SECOND WORLD WAR		
1946/47	Division Two	11th
1947/48	Division Two	19th
1948/49	Division Two	21st (relegated)
1949/50	Division Three (South)	4th
1950/51	Division Three (South)	1st (champions)
1951/52	Division Two	4th
1952/53	Division Two	7th
1953/54	Division Two	4th
1954/55	Division Two	15th
1955/56	Division Two	7th
1956/57	Division Two	2nd (promoted)
1957/58	Division One	10th
1958/59	Division One	13th
1959/60	Division One	20th
1960/61	Division One	14th

Season	Competition	Position
1961/62	Division One	19th
1962/63	Division One	9th
1963/64	Division One	13th
1964/65	Division One	5th
1965/66	Division One	18th
1966/67	Division One	2nd
1967/68	Division One	11th
1968/69	Division One	18th
1969/70	Division One	15th
1970/71	Division One	16th
1971/72	Division One	21st (relegated)
1972/73	Division Two	14th
1973/74	Division Two	7th
1974/75	Division Two	16th
1975/76	Division Two	8th
1976/77	Division Two	3rd (promoted)
1977/78	Division One	1st (champions)
1978/79	Division One	2nd
1979/80	Division One	5th
1980/81	Division One	7th
1981/82	Division One	12th
1982/83	Division One	5th
1983/84	Canon First Division	3rd
1984/85	Canon First Division	9th
1985/86	Canon First Division	8th
1986/87	Today First Division	8th
1987/88	Barclays First Division	3rd
1988/89	Barclays First Division	3rd
1989/90	Barclays First Division	9th
1990/91	Barclays First Division	8th
1991/92	Barclays First Division	8th
1992/93	FA Carling Premiership	22nd (relegated)
1993/94	Endsleigh Division One	2nd (promoted)
1994/95	FA Carling Premiership	3rd
1995/96	FA Carling Premiership	9th

Season	Competition	Position
1996/97	FA Carling Premiership	20th (relegated)
1997/98	Nationwide Division One	1st (champions)
1998/99	FA Carling Premiership	20th (relegated)
1999/2000	Nationwide Division One	14th
2000/01	Nationwide Division One	11th
2001/02	Nationwide Division One	16th
2002/03	Nationwide Division One	6th
2003/04	Nationwide Division One	14th
2004/05	Coca-Cola Championship	23rd (relegated)
2005/06	Coca-Cola League One	7th
2006/07	Coca-Cola League One	4th
2007/08	Coca-Cola League One	2nd (promoted)
2008/09	Coca-Cola Championship	19th
2009/10	Coca-Cola Championship	3rd
2010/11	Npower Championship	6th

NOTTINGHAM FOREST'S COMPLETE, SEASON-BY-SEASON FA CUP RECORD

SEASON	STAGE	RESULT
1878/79	SF	lost 2–1 to Old Etonians
1879/80	SF	lost 1–0 to Oxford University
1880/81	R2	lost 2–1 at home to Aston Villa
1881/82	R1	lost 4–1 away to Aston Villa
1882/83	R3	lost replay 3–2 away to Sheffield Wednesday after 2–2 at home
1883/84	R2	lost 3–0 away to Notts County
1884/85	SF	lost replay 3–0 to Queens Park after 1–1 (both at neutral grounds)
1885/86	R3	lost 2–1 away to Staveley
1886/87	R3	lost 2–1 away to Lockwood Brothers
1887/88	R5	lost 4–2 at home to Sheffield Wednesday

SEASON	STAGE	RESULT
1888/89	R2	lost second replay 3–2 away to Chatham after 1–1 away, and 2–2 home in the replay
1889/90	R1	lost 3–0 away to Derby Midland
1890/91	R3	lost 4–0 away to Sunderland
1891/92	SF	lost second replay 6–2 to West Bromwich Albion after 1–1, 1–1 in the replay (all at neutral grounds)
1892/93	R2	lost 4–2 away to Everton
1893/94	R3	lost replay 4–1 away to Notts County after 1–1 at home
1894/95	R3	lost 6–2 away to Aston Villa
1895/96	R1	lost 2–0 at home to Everton
1896/97	R3	lost replay 1–0 at home to Liverpool after 1–1 away
1897/98	Winners	Beat Derby County 3–1 at Crystal Palace
1898/99	R3	lost 1–0 at home to Sheffield United
1899/1900	SF	lost replay 3–2 to Bury after 1–1 in first game
1900/01	R2	lost 3–1 at home to Aston Villa
1901/02	SF	lost 3–1 to Southampton
1902/03	R2	lost replay 2–0 away to Stoke City after 0–0 at home
1903/04	R2	lost 3–1 away to Blackburn Rovers
1904/05	R2	lost 1–0 away to Fulham
1905/06	R3	lost 4–1 away to Sheffield Wednesday
1906/07	R2	lost replay 2–1 away to Barnsley after 1–1 at home
1907/08	R1	lost 2–0 away to Newcastle United
1908/09	R4	lost 3–0 away to Derby County
1909/10	R3	lost 3–1 away to Coventry City
1910/11	R1	lost 2–1 away to West Ham United
1911/12	R1	lost 1–0 at home to Bradford Park Avenue
1912/13	R2	lost 5–1 away to Oldham Athletic
1913/14	R1	lost replay 1–0 at home to Leyton Orient after 2–2 away
1914/15	R1	lost 4–1 at home to Norwich City

SEASON	STAGE	RESULT
		SUSPENDED OWING TO FIRST WORLD WAR
1919/20	R3	lost 3–0 away to Bradford Park Avenue
1920/21	R3	lost 2–0 away to Newcastle United after 1–1
1921/22	R5	lost 4–1 away to Cardiff City
1922/23	R3	lost third replay 1–0 to Sheffield United (on neutral ground) after 0–0 at home, 0–0 away (aet), and 1–1 (aet)
1923/24	R1	lost 2–0 away to Manchester City
1924/25	R2	lost 2–0 at home to West Ham United
1925/26	R6	lost second replay 1–0 to Bolton Wanderers after 2–2 at home, and 0–0 aet away
1926/27	R4	lost 2–0 away to Wolverhampton Wanderers
1927/28	R6	lost 3–0 away to Sheffield United
1928/29	R3	lost 2–1 at home to Swansea City
1929/30	R6	lost replay 3–1 away to Sheffield Wednesday after 2–2 at home
1930/31	R3	lost 4–0 away to Newcastle United
1931/32	R3	lost 5–2 away to Chesterfield
1932/33	R3	lost replay 2–1 at home to Bury after 2–2 away
1933/34	R4	lost replay 3–0 at home to Chelsea after 1–1 away
1934/35	R5	lost replay 3–0 away to Burnley after 0–0 at home
1935/36	R4	lost 2–0 away to Derby County
1936/37	R3	lost 4–2 at home to Sheffield United
1937/38	R4	lost 3–1 at home to Middlesbrough
1938/39	R3	lost replay 3–0 at home to Huddersfield Town after 0–0 away
		SUSPENDED OWING TO SECOND WORLD WAR
1945/46	R3	lost replay 1–0 at home to Watford after 1–1 away
1946/47	R5	lost replay 6–2 away to Middlesbrough after 2–2 at home
1947/48	R3	lost 4–1 away to Liverpool
1948/49	R3	lost replay 4–0 away to Liverpool after 2–2 at home

SEASON	STAGE	RESULT
1949/50	R2	lost 2–0 at home to Stockport County
1950/51	R2	lost 3–1 away to Rotherham United
1951/52	R3	lost replay 2–0 away to Blackburn Rovers after 2–2 at home
1952/53	R4	lost 4–1 away to Everton
1953/54	R3	lost 2–0 away to Plymouth Argyle
1954/55	R5	lost second replay 2–1 to Newcastle United after 1–1 at home, and 2–2 away
1955/56	R3	lost 3–0 away to Doncaster Rovers
1956/57	R6	lost replay 1–0 at home to Birmingham City after 0–0 away
1957/58	R4	lost replay 5–1 at home to West Bromwich Albion after 3–3 away draw
1958/59	Winners	Beat Luton Town 2–1 at Wembley
1959/60	R3	lost 3–0 away to Sheffield United
1960/61	R3	lost 2–0 at home to Birmingham City
1961/62	R4	lost 2–0 at home to Sheffield Wednesday
1962/63	R6	lost second replay 5–0 to Southampton after 1–1 at home, and 3–3 in replay
1963/64	R3	lost replay 1–0 away to Preston North End after 0–0 at home
1964/65	R5	lost 3–1 away to Crystal Palace
1965/66	R4	lost 2–0 away to Hull City
1966/67	SF	lost 2–1 to Tottenham Hotspur
1967/68	R4	lost 2–1 away to Leeds United
1968/69	R3	lost 3–0 away to Preston North End
1969/70	R3	lost 2–1 away to Carlisle United
1970/71	R5	lost 2–1 away to Tottenham Hotspur
1971/72	R3	lost 3–1 away to Millwall
1972/73	R3	lost second replay 3–1 to West Bromwich Albion after 1–1 away, and 0–0 at home
1973/74	R6	lost replay 1–0 away to Newcastle United after 0–0 home draw
1974/75	R4	lost third replay 2–1 to Fulham after 0–0 away, 1–1 home, and 1–1

SEASON	STAGE	RESULT
1975/76	R3	lost replay 1–0 away to Peterborough United after 0–0 at home
1976/77	R4	lost replay 2–1 away to Southampton after 3–3 at home
1977/78	R6	lost 2–0 away to West Bromwich Albion
1978/79	R5	lost 1–0 at home to Arsenal
1979/80	R4	lost 2–0 at home to Liverpool
1980/81	R6	lost replay 1–0 away to Ipswich Town after 3–3 at home
1981/82	R3	lost 3–1 at home to Wrexham
1982/83	R3	lost 2–0 away to Derby County
1983/84	R3	lost 2–1 at home to Southampton
1984/85	R4	lost replay 1–0 away to Wimbledon after 0–0 at home
1985/86	R3	lost replay 3–2 away to Blackburn Rovers after 1–1 at home
1986/87	R3	lost 1–0 away to Crystal Palace
1987/88	SF	lost 2–1 to Liverpool
1988/89	SF	lost replayed game 3–1 to Liverpool after first game at Hillsborough abandoned
1989/90	R3	lost 1–0 at home to Manchester United
1990/91	Final	lost 2–1 aet to Tottenham Hotspur
1991/92	R6	lost 1–0 away to Portsmouth
1992/93	R5	lost 2–0 away to Arsenal
1993/94	R3	lost replay 2–0 at home to Sheffield United after 1–1 away
1994/95	R4	lost 2–1 at home to Crystal Palace
1995/96	R6	lost 1–0 at home to Aston Villa
1996/97	R5	lost 1–0 away to Chesterfield
1997/98	R3	lost 4–1 away to Charlton Athletic
1998/99	R3	lost 1–0 at home to Portsmouth
1999/2000	R4	lost 2–0 away to Chelsea
2000/01	R3	lost 1–0 at home to Wolverhampton Wanderers
2001/02	R3	lost 1–0 away to Sheffield United

SEASON	STAGE	RESULT
2002/03	R3	lost 3–2 away to West Ham United
2003/04	R4	lost 3–0 at home to Sheffield United
2004/05	R5	lost replay 3–0 at home to Tottenham Hotspur after 1–1 away
2005/06	R2	lost 3–0 away to Chester City
2006/07	R4	lost 3–0 away to Chelsea
2007/08	R2	lost 1–0 away to Luton Town
2008/09	R4	lost replay 3–2 at home to Derby County after 1–1 away
2009/10	R3	lost replay 1–0 away to Birmingham City after 0–0 at home
2010/11	R4	lost 3–2 away to West Ham United

NOTTINGHAM FOREST'S COMPLETE SEASON-BY-SEASON LEAGUE CUP RECORD

SEASON	STAGE	RESULT
1960/61	R4	lost 2–1 away to Burnley
1961/62	R3	lost 2–1 at home to Blackburn Rovers
1962/63	–	Didn't compete
1963/64	–	Didn't compete
1964/65	–	Didn't compete
1965/66	–	Didn't compete
1966/67	R2	lost 2–1 away to Birmingham City after 1–1 at home
1967/68	R3	lost 2–0 away to Burnley
1968/69	R2	lost 3–2 at home to West Bromwich Albion
1969/70	R4	lost 1–0 at home to Oxford United
1970/71	R3	lost 2–1 away to Birmingham City
1971/72	R3	lost replay 2–1 away to Chelsea after 1–1 at home
1972/73	R2	lost 1–0 at home to Aston Villa
1973/74	R2	lost replay 3–1 at home to Millwall after 0–0 away

SEASON	STAGE	RESULT
1974/75	R2	lost replay 3–0 away to Newcastle United after 1–1 at home
1975/76	R3	lost 2–1 away to Manchester City
1976/77	R3	lost 3–0 at home to Coventry City
1977/78	Winners	beat Liverpool 1–0 in a replay at Old Trafford after 0–0 aet at Wembley
1978/79	Winners	beat Southampton 3–2 at Wembley
1979/80	Final	lost 1–0 to Wolves at Wembley
1980/81	R4	lost 4–1 away to Watford
1981/82	R5	lost 1–0 away to Tottenham Hotspur
1982/83	R5	lost 4–0 away to Manchester United
1983/84	R2	lost to Wimbledon 3–1 on aggregate, after losing 2–0 away and drawing 1–1 at home
1984/85	R3	lost replay 1–0 aet away to Sunderland after 1–1 at home
1985/86	R4	lost 3–1 away to Queens Park Rangers
1986/87	R5	lost 2–0 away to Arsenal
1987/88	R3	lost 3–0 away to Manchester City
1988/89	Winners	beat Luton Town 3–1 at Wembley
1989/90	Winners	beat Oldham Athletic 1–0 at Wembley
1990/91	R4	lost 5–4 away to Coventry City
1991/92	Final	lost 1–0 to Manchester United at Wembley
1992/93	R5	lost 2–0 away to Arsenal
1993/94	R5	lost replay 2–0 away to Tranmere Rovers after 1–1 at home
1994/95	R4	lost 2–1 at home to Millwall
1995/96	R2	lost to Bradford City 5–4 on aggregate, after losing 3–2 away and drawing 2–2 at home
1996/97	R3	lost 4–1 away to West Ham United
1997/98	R2	lost to Walsall 3–2 on aggregate, after losing 1–0 at home and drawing 2–2 away
1998/99	R4	lost 2–1 away to Manchester United
1999/2000	R3	lost 4–1 away to Sheffield Wednesday
2000/01	R1	lost to Darlington 4–3 on aggregate, after drawing 2–2 away and losing 2–1 at home

SEASON	STAGE	RESULT
2001/02	R3	lost 1–0 away to Bolton Wanderers
2002/03	R2	lost 2–1 at home to Walsall
2003/04	R3	lost 4–2 aet at home to Portsmouth
2004/05	R4	lost 4–2 aet at home to Luton Town
2005/06	R1	lost 3–2 at home to Macclesfield Town
2006/07	R1	lost 3–0 away to Accrington Stanley
2007/08	R2	lost 3–2 at home to Leicester City
2008/09	R2	lost 2–1 at home to Sunderland
2009/10	R3	lost 1–0 at home to Blackburn Rovers
2010/11	R1	lost 2–1 aet away to Bradford City

NUREMBERG TOURNAMENT WINNERS

Forest won this trophy in 1982 after beating Dukla Prague and Nuremberg.

Forest beat Dukla Prague 2–0
Forest: Sutton; Anderson, Bowyer; Aas, Young, Proctor (Hodge); Plummer, Wallace (Davenport), Fashanu, Walsh, Robertson
Scorers for Forest: Robertson (penalty), Walsh

Forest beat Nuremberg 4–2
Forest: Sutton; Anderson (Gunn), Bowyer; Proctor, Young (Fairclough), Todd; Plummer, Davenport, Fashanu, Walsh, Robertson
Scorers for Forest: Walsh, Davenport, Robertson, Plummer

PLAYER OF THE YEAR

Kenny Burns won the accolade of Football Writers' Association Player of the Year in 1977/78.

FOREST LEGEND – PETER SHILTON MBE, CBE

An outstanding, world-class goalkeeper, Shilts joined Forest from Stoke City for a fee of £270,000 in September 1977, after making 110 league appearances for the Potters. Shilton made his debut for Forest in the 2–0 defeat of Aston Villa at the City Ground on 17 September 1977, going on to make 202 league appearances for the Reds. The PFA's 1978 Player of the Year was undoubtedly one of the best goalkeepers ever to pull on a jersey. Shilton was also honoured with the PFA Merit Award in 1990. A member of Forest's league- and two successful European Cup-winning teams, Peter was born in Leicester on 18 September 1949, joining the Foxes as an apprentice in September 1966, where he made 286 league appearances (including one in the Foxes' losing cup final team in 1969). He even scored, yes, scored, 1 goal, before transferring to Stoke City for £325,000.

He made his England debut against East Germany on 25 November 1970, and won his last cap in July 1990, winning a record 125 caps for an England goalkeeper. It would surely have been many more had not 61 cap-winning Ray Clemence been around at the same time. Shilts played for England in the finals of three World Cups and two European Championships. Added to the above are 3 under-23 caps, plus a number for the England youth side. He left Forest for Southampton for £300,000 in August 1982, making 188 league appearances for the Saints. In July 1987 he transferred to Derby County for £90,000, making 175 league appearances for the Rams. Following a brief spell as player-manager at Plymouth Argyle then Wimbledon as a non-contract player (where he made no appearances), he then went to Bolton Wanderers where he made 1 substitute appearance. He joined Coventry in July 1995, then West Ham in January 1996, but made no appearances for either club. He finally signed for Leyton Orient in November 1996, where he played 9 times. A short spell at Middlesbrough heralded the end of his long and illustrious career, and Peter finally hung up his gloves. While at Orient, Peter made his record-breaking 1,000th league appearance, the first and, to date, only player in the history of the game to reach this milestone. This televised game was Orient against Brighton in December 1996. In all, including 125 internationals, Shilts played in 1,375 senior games, 1,005 of those being league appearances. In 2010 Peter Shilton was seen tripping the light fantastic on BBC1's *Strictly Come Dancing*.

PLAY-OFFS

To date Nottingham Forest have been involved in four play-offs:

Championship 2002/03. Forest finished 6th in the league, but lost the play-off semi-final to Sheffield United 5–4 on aggregate after drawing the first leg 1–1 and losing the second leg 4–3.

League One 2006/07. Forest finished 4th in the league, but lost the play-off semi-final to Yeovil Town 5–4 on aggregate after wining the first leg 2–0 and losing the second leg 5–2 after extra time.

Championship 2009/10. Forest finished 3rd in the league, but lost the play-off semi-final to Blackpool 6–4 on aggregate after losing the first leg 2–1 and the second leg 4–3.

Championship 2010/11. Forest finished 6th in the league but lost the play-off semi-final to Swansea 3–0 on aggregate after drawing the first leg 0–0 at the City Ground and losing the second leg 3–0.

FOREST LEGEND – PETER TAYLOR

Wily fox Peter Taylor was the calming influence that Brian Clough needed. Born in Nottingham on 2 July 1928, Taylor made 86 league appearances in goal for Coventry City, signing for the Sky Blues in May 1946 after being on Forest's books as an amateur. In August 1955 he was transferred to Middlesbrough, where he made 140 league appearances, before moving to Port Vale in June 1961, playing in only 1 league game. He subsequently joined Southern League Burton Albion. It was at Middlesbrough that Taylor first met Brian Clough, the old stager and the young pretender becoming firm friends. In October 1962, Taylor became manager of Burton Albion, winning the Southern League Cup with the Eton Park club in 1963/64. In October 1965, Clough persuaded Taylor to join him at Hartlepool as his assistant, and from there they moved to Second Division Derby County in June 1967, where they won promotion as champions in 1968/69. Their first Division One championship came in 1971/72, reaching the semi-finals of the European Cup the following season. The duo resigned in October 1973, and a month later Taylor followed Clough to Brighton as assistant manager. Taylor took over as manager of Brighton in June 1974 after Cloughie had taken the ill-fated 44-day long Leeds job, guiding the Seagulls to fourth spot in Division Three in 1975/76. Peter Taylor once again joined his long-time partner, this time in July 1976, at Nottingham Forest. Another trophy-laden period followed, ending when Taylor announced his retirement at the end of the 1981/82 season. At Wembley on 17 March 1979, Peter Taylor proudly led out the Forest team for the 1979 League Cup final, in which Forest beat Southampton 3–2. Subsequently, Peter Taylor returned to football management on 11 August 1982 with Second Division Derby County. After Taylor poached Robbo in 1983 while Cloughie was away on one of his charity fundraising trips – walking the Pennine Way – the relationship between the one-time partners and friends dipped into a stubborn feud that sadly never ended. Peter Taylor left Derby on 4 April 1984, and the Rams were relegated at the end of that 1983/84 season. The world of football lost one of its characters when Peter Taylor died in his Majorcan villa in October 1990.

RECORDS

Biggest Away Win
Apart from Forest's away 14–0 demolition of Clapton in the FA Cup on 17 January 1891, there have been two 7–1 away wins:

Port Vale 1–7 Forest, Division Two, 2 February 1957
Sheffield Wednesday 1–7 Forest, Premier League, 1 April 1995

Biggest Home Win
Forest 12–0 Leicester City, Division One, 21 April 1909

Biggest Away Defeat
Blackburn Rovers 9–1 Forest, Division Two, 10 April 1937
Tottenham 9–2 Forest, Division One, 29 September 1962

Also Forest have been beaten 8–0 on four occasions:

West Bromwich Albion 8–0 Forest, Division One, 16 April 1900
Leeds City 8–0 Forest, Division Two, 29 November 1913
Birmingham City 8–0 Forest, Division Two, 10 March 1920
Burnley 8–0 Forest, Division One, 21 November 1959

Biggest Home Defeat
Forest 1–8 Man United, Premier League, 6 February 1999

Record Attendance
49,946 v Man United in Division One, 28 October 1967

Record Receipts

£499,099 versus Bayern Munich in UEFA Cup quarter-final, second leg, 19 March 1996

Longest Sequence of League wins

Forest have won seven successive games on four occasions, although one of these was over two seasons:

Division One, from 24 December 1892 to 25 February 1893: Wolves (h) 3–1, Blackburn (a) 1–0, Accrington (h) 3–0, Everton (h) 2–1, Man Utd (a) 3–1, Derby (h) 1–0, Notts County (h) 3–1

Division Two, from 20 October 1906 to 1 December 1906: Leyton Orient (h) 4–0, Gainsborough Trinity (a) 3–2, Stockport (h) 2–1, Hull (a) 2–1, Glossop North End (h) 2–0, Blackpool (a) 2–1, Bradford City (h) 3–0

1906/07 was also notable because after Forest were beaten 4–2 by Port Vale on 5 January 1907, the Reds went the rest of the season unbeaten: 17 games in all, including 15 wins and 2 draws.

Division Two, 29 August 1921 to 1 October 1921: Hull (h) 3–2, Crystal Palace (h) 2–1, Hull (a) 1–0, Coventry (a) 1–0, Coventry (h) 1–0, Derby (a) 2–1, Derby (h) 3–0

Division One, from 9 May 1979 to 1 September 1979: In season 1978/79: Man City (h) 3–1, Leeds (a) 2–1, WBA (a) 1–0 In season 1979/80: Ipswich (a) 1–0, Stoke (h) 1–0, Coventry (h) 4–1, WBA (a) 5–1. This sequence of victories was followed by a 0–0 draw at Leeds United.

Longest sequence of League Defeats

Forest lost 14 Division Two games spanning two seasons, from 21 March 1913, in season 1912/13 (where Forest lost their final 8 games), to 27 September 1913 in season 1913/14 (where Forest lost their first 6 games). Forest ended the 1913/14 season at the foot of the table.

Longest Sequence of League Draws

Forest drew 7 Division One games on the trot spanning two seasons, from 29 April 1978 where Forest drew their final 3 games in 1977/78, to 2 September 1978, Forest drawing their first 4 games of 1978/79.

Longest Sequence of Unbeaten League Matches

Division One, 42 games unbeaten, from 26 November 1977 to 25 November 1978

Longest Sequence Without a League Win

Premier League, 1998/99, 19 games from 8 September 1998 to 16 January 1999. Forest finally ended this sequence with a 1–0 victory away at Everton.

Most League Appearances

Bob McKinlay, 614, between 1951 and 1970

Most Capped Player

Stuart Pearce, 78 for England, 76 while playing for Forest

First Football League Game

Saturday 3 September 1892, Division One versus Everton away, result 2–2

First Home Football League Game

Saturday 10 September 1892, versus Stoke, Forest lost 4–3

First Home Football League Victory
Thursday 20 October 1892, Forest 2–0 Bolton

First Football League Victory
Saturday 1 October 1892, away, Forest beat Derby 2–0

Most Clean Sheets
Forest have achieved the feat of six games with a clean sheet on two occasions:

Division Two, from 26 November 1921 to 26 December 1921: 4 wins and 2 draws. Division One, from 19 April 1980 to 9 May 1980: 4 wins and 2 draws

Most League Points in a Season
70 points in Division Three (South), 1950/51 (2 points for a win): 40 games, 30 wins, 10 draws, 6 defeats, goals scored 110, goals conceded 40. Forest's final 8 games were unbeaten: 7 wins and 1 draw

94 points in Division 1, 1997/98 (3 points for a win): 46 games, 28 wins, 10 draws, 8 defeats, 82 goals scored, 42 goals conceded. Forest's final 7 games were unbeaten: 5 wins and 2 draws

Most League Goals Scored in One Season
110 goals scored in Division Three (South), 1950/51

Highest League Scorer in One Season
Wally Ardron – 36 goals in Division Three (South), 1950/51

Most League Goals Scored
Grenville Morris – 199 goals from 1898 to 1913

Most League Goals from One Player in One Match

Four goals have been scored by one player in one game eleven times by a total of eight players (Tom Peacock netting four on four separate occasions – three of which in the same season):

9 Nov 1907	Enoch West v Sunderland (H)
12 Jan 1913	Tommy Gibson v Burnley (A)
23 Dec 1933	Tom Peacock v Port Vale (H)
9 Nov 1935	Tom Peacock v Barnsley (H)
23 Nov 1935	Tom Peacock v Port Vale (H)
26 Dec 1935	Tom Peacock v Doncaster Rovers (H)
18 Nov 1950	Tommy Capel v Gillingham (H)
26 Dec 1952	Wally Ardron v Hull City (A)
9 Feb 1957	Tommy Wilson v Barnsley (H)
4 Oct 1977	Peter Withe v Ipswich Town (H)
22 Feb 2003	Marlon Harewood v Stoke City (H)

Record Transfers

Out: Stan Collymore, £8.5 million to Liverpool
In: Pierre van Hooijdonk, £4.5 million from Celtic

Highest Home Scoring Draw

Nottingham Forest 4–4 West Bromwich Albion, Division One, 28 October 1961

Highest Away Scoring Draw

Forest have drawn 3–3 away from home on numerous occasions in the League; too many to list.

Highest FA Cup Away Scoring Draws

West Bromwich Albion 3–3 Nottingham Forest, FA Cup, round four, 25 January 1958

Southampton 3–3 Nottingham Forest, FA Cup, round six replay, 3 April 1963, Forest lost the second replay 5–0.

Highest League Cup Away Scoring Draws
Huddersfield Town 3–3 Nottingham Forest, League Cup, round two, second leg, 3 October 1989, 4–4 (aet), Forest won on the away goals rule.

Wrexham 3–3 Nottingham Forest, League Cup, round two, first leg, 21 September 1993, Forest won the home leg 3–1, and the tie 6–4 on aggregate.

Highest FA Cup Home Scoring Draws
Nottingham Forest 3–3 Sunderland Albion, FA Cup, round two replay, 7 February 1891

Nottingham Forest 3–3 Southampton, FA Cup, round four, 29 January 1977

Nottingham Forest 3–3 Bolton Wanderers, FA Cup, round three, 3 January 1981

Nottingham Forest 3–3 Ipswich Town, FA Cup, round six, 7 March 1981

Highest League Cup Home Score Draws
Nottingham Forest 3–3 Cambridge United, League Cup, round three, 27 October 1998 aet, Forest won on penalties.

Highest Away FA Cup Defeat
West Bromwich Albion 6–2 Nottingham Forest, FA Cup, semi-final, 9 March 1892

Aston Villa 6–2 Nottingham Forest, FA Cup, round three, 2 March 1895

Middlesbrough 6–2 Nottingham Forest, FA Cup, round five replay, 29 February 1947

Highest Away League Cup Score
Doncaster Rovers 0–8 Nottingham Forest, League Cup, round one, 11 August 1997

Lowest attendance
At the City Ground: 2,013 versus Brentford, Football League Trophy, 31 October 2006

CLOUGHIE ON MAN UTD AND FERGIE

'Manchester United in Brazil? I hope they all get bloody diarrhoea.'
  Cloughie's comment when Manchester United chose to play in the World Club Championship rather than in the FA Cup

'For all his horses, knighthoods and championships, he hasn't got two of what I've got. And I don't mean balls.'
  Cloughie's scathing judgement on Alex Ferguson's failure to win two European Cups

REPUBLIC OF IRELAND INTERNATIONALS

The three most notable Irish international footballers who played for Nottingham Forest (although not all caps came when they played for the club) are:

Roy Keane   62 caps
Andy Reid   27 caps
Miah Dennehy   11 caps

RESERVES

Nottingham Forest's reserve team play in the Central League, currently known as the Totesport.com League. Originally founded in 1911 it consisted in its early years of a mixture of first teams as well as reserve teams. In 1921 when the Third Division North was formed, every one of the Central League's first teams transferred into that new league, leaving the Central League to comprise solely of reserve teams. These days there is a separate FA Premier Reserve League.

Nottingham Forest have won the Central League on four occasions: 1987/88, 1988/89, 1991/92 and 2006/07 following victory in the play-offs, the league having been split into three geographic divisions in 2005. In 2007/08 Forest won the Division One Central division, but lost in the play-offs; the eventual winner that season being Manchester City. Since 2008 the play-off system has been replaced and now the winner is the side with the season's best points per game record. Liverpool have won the Central League 16 times, second are Manchester United with 6 wins.

SCOTLAND INTERNATIONALS

Scotland has produced many fine international players. Among the most notable who played for Nottingham Forest during their career (though not all caps came when they were at the club) are:

Archie Gemmill	43 caps
Frank Gray	32 caps
John Robertson	28 caps
Scot Gemmill	26 caps
Kenny Burns	20 caps
Peter Cormack	9 caps
Gareth Williams	5 caps

FOREST LEGEND – SAM WIDDOWSON

Born in Hucknall Torkard on 16 April 1851, Sam Weller Widdowson is an undisputed legendary figure in the sporting history of Nottinghamshire. A great all-round athlete, sprinter, swimmer and oarsman, he also played football for Nottingham Forest and cricket for Nottinghamshire. The sporting world owes a number of debts to Sam Widdowson. This giant of cricket and football is the acclaimed inventor of shin-pads, having used his cut-down cricket pads when playing football for Nottingham Forest. At that time 'hacking' – the deliberate kicking of an opponent's shins – was prevalent in the English game. In those days (Forest joined the Sheffield Association in 1868) hacking was allowed under the code known as the 'Sheffield Rules' which permitted players to deliberately kick the shins of their opponents. Because no one wore protection it was common for players to end a game with their shins covered in bruises. Although primitive, Sam Widdowson's protective devices were effective enough to be adopted and developed into the high-tech descendants of today.

Following the Royal Engineers football team's 1873 tour of the north (during which they beat Forest 2–1), Sam Widdowson, captain of Forest, was inspired by their impressive style of football to come up with a 'new revolutionary' playing formation to replace the old 'loose' kick-and-rush style favoured by northern teams. This consisted of a goalkeeper, two backs, one half-back and seven attackers. Widdowson is credited with the inventing and implementation of the first organised team formation of: no. 1 goalkeeper, two full-backs (2 – right-back, 3 – left-back), three half-backs (4 – right half, 5 – centre half/pivot, 6 – left half) and five forwards (7 – right-wing, or outside right, 8 – inside right, 9 – centre-forward, 10 – inside-left, 11 – left-wing, or outside left).

Sam Widdowson was a member of the Forest Football Club Committee for many years, representing the club at the inaugural meeting of the Football League in 1888 where

Forest wished to stay solidly amateur, not pursuing the professional dream. He was also an England selector, and is credited with having refereed the first game where goal nets were used.

SECRETARIES OF NOTTINGHAM FOREST

1865–66	J.S. Milford
1866–68	W.R. Lymberry
1868–88	H.S. Radford
1888–89	C.A. Rastall
1889–97	H.B. Radford
1897–1909	H. Hallam
1909–12	F.W. Earp
1912–25	R.G. Marsters
1925–29	J.H. Baynes
1929–31	S. Hardy
1931–61	G.N. Watson
1961–86	K. Smales
1987–	P. White

SPONSORS

Victor Chandler	2009–
Capital One	2003–09
Pinnacle	1997–2003
Labatts	1992–97
Shipstones	1987–91
Home Ales	1986–87
Skol	1984–86
Wrangler	1983–84
Panasonic	1981–83

STRIKERS/GOALSCORERS

Nottingham Forest fans, like those of every club in the world, love goals and the players who score them. Here's a non-definitive list of ten Forest goalscorers/strikers/centre-forwards/inside forwards, their goals, appearances including those as substitute, and their ratio of goals to games for the club:

Grenville Morris	217 goals from 460 appearances	1 in 2.12
Nigel Clough	131 goals from 412 appearances	1 in 3.15
Wally Ardron	124 goals from 191 appearances	1 in 1.54
Johnny Dent	122 goals from 206 appearances	1 in 1.69
Enoch West	100 goals from 183 appearances	1 in 1.83
Garry Birtles	96 goals from 283 appearances	1 in 2.95
Tommy Wilson	90 goals from 217 appearances	1 in 2.41
Tommy Capel	72 goals from 162 appearances	1 in 2.25
Jim Barrett	69 goals from 117 appearances	1 in 1.70

By comparison, here are a few others you may recognise:

Tony Woodcock	62 goals from 180 appearances	1 in 2.90
Peter Davenport	58 goals from 147 appearances	1 in 2.53
Johnny Quigley	58 goals from 270 appearances	1 in 2.93
Marlon Harewood	55 goals from 207 appearances	1 in 3.76
Frank Wignall	53 goals from 179 appearances	1 in 3.38
Stan Collymore	50 goals from 77+1 appearances	1 in 1.56
David Johnson	50 goals from 168 appearances	1 in 3.36
Joe Baker	49 goals from 135 appearances	1 in 2.76
P. van Hooijdonk	41 goals from 72+5 appearances	1 in 1.88
Peter Withe	39 goals from 99 appearances	1 in 2.54

GOALSCORING MIDFIELDERS/ INSIDE FORWARDS

Driving their teams on from the middle of the park while scoring lots of goals were the following six:

Ian Bowyer	96 goals from 564 appearances	1 in 5.88
Colin Addison	69 goals from 176 appearances	1 in 2.55
Steve Hodge	66 goals from 273 appearances	1 in 4.14
Neil Webb	63 goals from 229 appearances	1 in 3.63
Noah Burton	62 goals from 320 appearances	1 in 5.16
Tom Peacock	62 goals from 120 appearances	1 in 1.94

GOALSCORING WINGERS

Forest have been fortunate to have a good number of wingers who definitely knew where the net was. At times it could be argued that these players played some games in a more striking role. Here are the top five:

Ian Storey-Moore	118 goals from 272 appearances	1 in 2.31
John Robertson	95 goals from 514 appearances	1 in 5.41
Cyril Stocks	80 goals from 257 appearances	1 in 3.21
Bill Dickinson	73 goals from 143 appearances	1 in 1.96
Martin O'Neill	62 goals from 371 appearances	1 in 5.98

GOALSCORING DEFENDERS

Streets ahead of every other Forest defender is one man – Psycho:

Stuart Pearce	88 goals from 522 appearances	1 in 5.93

SUM TOTAL

According to the statto.com compilation of every league result from inception up to (and including) 13 May 2011, Nottingham Forest come in at number 18. At the top are:

Manchester United
Liverpool
Arsenal
Wolverhampton Wanderers

In all Forest have played 4,402 League games.

Forest's Home League Games

Pld	Won	Drawn	Lost	F	A	GD
2201	1114	558	529	3812	2417	+1395

Forest's Away League Games

Pld	Won	Drawn	Lost	F	A	GD
2201	544	573	1084	2571	3799	-1228

Forest's Total League Games

Pld	Won	Drawn	Lost	F	A	GD
4402	1658	1131	1613	6383	6216	+167

Forest statistics in the FA Cup (27th place)

Pld	Won	Drawn	Lost	F	A	GD
371	156	95	120	601	478	+123

Forest statistics in the League Cup (6th place)

Pld	Won	Drawn	Lost	F	A	GD
181	92	43	46	345	204	+141

THE DYNAMIC DUO'S TIMELINE

The Dynamic Duo first met at Middlesbrough and became friends. In the summer of 1965, Brian Clough was offered the manager's job at Hartlepool United, and the rest, as they say, is history.

October 1965	30-year-old Brian Clough appointed manager of Fourth Division Hartlepool United, making him the youngest manager in the Football League.
October 1965	Peter Taylor joins Hartlepool as assistant manager.
June 1967	The 'Duo' move to Second Division Derby County.
1968/69	Derby win the Second Division championship.
1971/72	Derby win the First Division championship.
1972/73	Derby reach the semi-finals of the European Cup.
October 1973	Clough and Taylor resign from Derby.
November 1973	Clough and Taylor join Brighton.
July 1974	Clough resigns to join Leeds, Taylor stays at Brighton as manager.
44 days later	Clough is sacked by Leeds.
January 1975	Clough joins Second Division Forest.
July 1976	Taylor leaves Brighton and joins Clough at Nottingham Forest.
1976/77	Forest finish third in Division Two and win promotion.
1977/78	Forest win the First Division championship and the League Cup.
May 1978	Brian Clough named 'Manager of the Year'.
February 1979	Clough signs the first £1 million player, Trevor Francis from Birmingham.

1978/79	Forest finish second in the league, win the European Cup and the League Cup.
1979/80	Forest end the season fifth in the league, and win the European Cup for the second time. Sadly, the dream of three successive League Cup triumphs is shattered when Forest are beaten 1–0 by Wolves in the final at Wembley.
1980/81	Forest finish seventh in the league, and reach the sixth round of the FA Cup. They are knocked out of the League Cup in round four, and the European Cup in round one.
1981/82	Forest finish twelfth in the league, knocked out of FA Cup in round one, and League Cup in round five. Taylor retires at the end of the season. On 5 May, he told Clough he'd had enough.
11 August 1982	Taylor appointed manager of Second Division Derby County.
1982/83	Forest finish fifth in the league, knocked out in round one of the FA Cup by Derby, and round five of the League Cup. Derby finish thirteenth in Division Two.
1983/84	Forest finish third in Division One, and reach semi-finals of UEFA Cup.
June 1983	Clough and Taylor fall out after Taylor signs John Robertson for Derby while Clough was away on a charity walk.
4 April 1984	With his team facing relegation to Division Three, Taylor leaves Derby County after 62 games in charge, and retires from football.
1987/88	Forest reach the semi-finals of the FA Cup, losing to Liverpool. They finish third in Division One and are knocked out of League Cup in round three.

February 1989   Clough is charged with bringing the game into disrepute, and is fined £5,000 and banned from the touchline of all Football League grounds for the rest of the season.

1988/89   Forest win the League Cup, beating Luton Town 3–1 in the final, and reach the semi-finals of the FA Cup. On 15 April 1989 the tragedy at Hillsborough causes the game to be abandoned after 6 minutes. Forest lose the replay 3–1 to Liverpool on 7 May 1989 and finish third in Division One.

1989/90   Forest win the League Cup for the fourth time by beating Oldham Athletic 1–0. They are knocked out of the FA Cup in round one and finish ninth in the league.

October 1990   Peter Taylor dies.

1990/91   Forest reach the final of the FA Cup, only to lose 2–1 to Spurs. They finish eighth in the league and are knocked out of League Cup in Round 4.

1991/92   Forest reach the final of the League Cup only to lose 1–0 to Manchester United. They are knocked out of the FA Cup in round six and finish eighth in the league.

March 1993   Brian Clough receives the Freedom of the City of Nottingham.

1992/93   Forest finish bottom of the league and are relegated to Division Two. They are knocked out of FA Cup and the League Cup in the fifth round of each.

May 1993   Brian Clough resigns from Forest, and retires from football.

May 2003   Brian Clough receives the Freedom of the City of Derby.

| 20 September 2004 | The world was shocked to hear the sad announcement that Brian Clough had died of stomach cancer in Derby City Hospital at the age of 69. |

FOREST LEGEND – TOMMY CAPEL

Thomas 'Tommy' Capel was born in Chorlton, Manchester, on 27 June 1922, playing for Droylsden FC, Manchester City, Chesterfield and Birmingham City before being transferred to Forest in November 1949. He scored 72 goals for the Reds in 162 appearances between 1949 and 1954.

TIME GENTLEMEN

Cloughie is well-known for his infamous message to the more 'colourful' vocal Forest fans, written on a placard: 'Gentlemen, no swearing please. Brian'. Cloughie threatened to resign if the fans didn't tone down their language. The fans replied with their own placard, on which the message said: 'Brian, no leaving please. The Gentlemen'.

TAKE THAT

At the end of Forest's triumphant League Cup quarter-final victory over Queens Park Rangers in February 1989, Brian Clough got so incensed at the fans' pitch invasion that he lashed out, striking several fans. He was subsequently fined £5,000 for bringing the game into disrepute, and banned from the touchline of all Football League grounds for the rest of the season. Cloughie being Cloughie subsequently gave the reconciled lads a kiss.

FOREST LEGEND – TOMMY WILSON

Born in Bedlington on 15 September 1930, centre-forward Tommy Wilson banged in 90 goals for the Reds in 217 appearances, having joined Forest in April 1951. Tommy scored the winner against Luton Town in the 1959 FA Cup final.

UNBEATEN RECORD

Nottingham Forest's outstanding unbeaten record, held for 26 years, of 42 consecutive league games without defeat was finally beaten by Arsène Wenger's Arsenal. Arsenal's 5–3 victory over Middlesbrough on 21 August 2004 brought them level with Brian Clough's double European Cup-winning team. And in their match against Blackburn on 25 August, they beat the record with a convincing 3–0 victory.

Forest's record run was between 26 November 1977 and 25 November 1978. They won half and drew half of their 42 games in the run compared to Arsenal's 30 wins and 12 draws. Arsenal are also ahead in goals scored – a massive 92 to Forest's 58. However, Forest were tighter at the back, conceding just 22 goals compared to Arsenal's 31.

Forest's 42-game run was completed over two seasons, 26 in the 1977/78 title-winning season and 16 in the following campaign. It started with a 0–0 draw against West Bromwich Albion at the City Ground, and ended almost exactly a year later at Anfield when Liverpool beat Forest 2–0. One of the highlights of the run was the 4–0 victory over Manchester United at Old Trafford. United were at the time were languishing in the bottom half of the table and Forest ripped them to shreds. Tony Woodcock produced a great performance, scoring twice. John Robertson got another and the fourth was a Greenhoff own-goal.

Forest finished as league champions in the 1977/78 season, clinching it with four matches to go. At the home game against

Birmingham they were presented with the championship trophy for the first time in the club's 114-year history. At the end of the season they were 7 points ahead of rivals Liverpool with 64 points.

The players involved in the run are among the great names of Nottingham Forest's football history (in alphabetical order):

Anderson, Barrett, Birtles, Bowyer, Burns, Clark, Elliott, Gemmill, Lloyd, McGovern, Mills, Needham, O'Hare, O'Neill, Robertson, Shilton, Withe, Woodcock

Although not playing in the League, Forest's young keeper Chris Woods played an important part in Forest's League Cup run. At 18 he became the youngest goalkeeper to play in a Wembley final and he won his medal in the replay at Old Trafford when Forest lifted the League Cup.

Nottingham Forest's 42-Game Unbeaten Run

1977/78 season

Game	Date	Opponent	Venue	Result
1	Sat 26 Nov	West Bromwich Albion	Home	D 0–0
2	Sat 3 Dec	Birmingham City	Away	W 2–0
3	Sat 10 Dec	Coventry City	Home	W 2–1
4	Sat 17 Dec	Manchester United	Away	W 4–0
5	Mon 26 Dec	Liverpool	Home	D 1–1
6	Wed 28 Dec	Newcastle United	Away	W 2–0
7	Sat 31 Dec	Bristol City	Away	W 3–1
8	Mon 2 Jan	Everton	Home	D 1–1
9	Sat 14 Jan	Derby County	Away	D 0–0
10	Sat 21 Jan	Arsenal	Home	W 2–0
11	Sat 4 Feb	Wolves	Home	W 2–0
12	Sat 25 Feb	Norwich City	Away	D 3–3
13	Sat 4 Mar	West Ham United	Home	W 2–0
14	Tue 14 Mar	Leicester City	Home	W 1–0

15	Sat 25 Mar	Newcastle United	Home	W 2–0
16	Wed 29 Mar	Middlesbrough	Away	D 2–2
17	Sat 1 Apr	Chelsea	Home	W 3–1
18	Wed 5 Apr	Aston Villa	Away	W 1–0
19	Tue 11 Apr	Manchester City	Away	D 0–0
20	Sat 15 Apr	Leeds United	Home	D 1–1
21	Tue 18 Apr	Queens Park Rangers	Home	W 1–0
22	Sat 22 Apr	Coventry City	Away	D 0–0
23	Tue 25 Apr	Ipswich Town	Away	W 2–0
24	Sat 29 Apr	Birmingham City	Home	D 0–0
25	Tue 2 May	West Bromwich Albion	Away	D 2–2
26	Thu 4 May	Liverpool	Away	D 0–0

1978/79 season

Game	Date	Opponent	Venue	Result
27	Sat 19 Aug	Tottenham Hotspur	Home	D 1–1
28	Tue 22 Aug	Coventry City	Away	D 0–0
29	Sat 26 Aug	Queens Park Rangers	Away	D 0–0
30	Sat 2 Sep	West Bromwich Albion	Home	D 0–0
31	Sat 9 Sep	Arsenal	Home	W 2–1
32	Sat 16 Sep	Manchester United	Away	D 1–1
33	Sat 23 Sep	Middlesbrough	Home	D 2–2
34	Sat 30 Sep	Aston Villa	Away	W 2–1
35	Sat 7 Oct	Wolves	Home	W 3–1
36	Sat 14 Oct	Bristol City	Away	W 3–1
37	Sat 21 Oct	Ipswich Town	Home	W 1–0
38	Sat 28 Oct	Southampton	Away	D 0–0
39	Sat 4 Nov	Everton	Home	D 0–0
40	Sat 11 Nov	Tottenham Hotspur	Away	W 3–1
41	Sat 18 Nov	Queens Park Rangers	Home	D 0–0
42	Sat 25 Nov	Bolton Wanderers	Away	W 1–0

Sadly, Forest's unbeaten run ended on 9 December 1978 when Liverpool defeated them 2–0 at Anfield.

FOREST LEGEND – VIV ANDERSON MBE

Viv Anderson was born in Nottingham on 29 August 1956 and joined Forest straight from school as an apprentice in November 1972. He made his senior debut aged 18 on 21 September 1974 against Sheffield Wednesday, the first of 430 first-team outings, including 5 as substitute. In August 1984 he transferred to Arsenal for £250,000 where he made 120 League appearances. He subsequently moved to Manchester United, playing 54 league games for the Red Devils, and then on to Sheffield Wednesday on a free transfer. Viv played for the Owls in the 1993 FA Cup final, losing the replay 2–1 to Arsenal after a 1–1 draw. A member of the Forest side that won the European Cup in 1979 and 1980, the highly rated full-back was the first black player to represent England. He made his international debut in the 1–0 win over Czechoslovakia at Wembley on 29 November 1978. He went on to win 30 full England caps, to add to his single under-21 cap, scoring 2 goals for his country. He played for England in the 1980 European Championship finals alongside ex-Forest team-mate Tony Woodcock. At the end of his playing career, he had a short spell as player-manager of Barnsley, before becoming assistant manager to Bryan Robson at Middlesbrough. Awarded an MBE in January 2000, he was inducted into the English Football Hall of Fame in 2004 in recognition of his impact on English football. These days Viv Anderson is a consultant, an FA goodwill ambassador and presenter on MUTV, as well as working for charity.

WARTIME DISASTER

England defender Billy Wright once scored a dramatic hat-trick for Wolves in the space of 21 minutes against Forest in February 1946, during a wartime Football League (South) game. Ray Chatham got the other goal for Wolves in a 4–0 defeat.

WALES INTERNATIONALS

Quite a number of Welsh cap winners have played for Nottingham Forest during their career, here are a few (not all caps won while at the club):

Dean Saunders	75 caps	Grenville Morris	21 caps
David Phillips	62 caps	Andy Johnson	15 caps
Robert Earnshaw	51 caps	Gareth Taylor	15 caps
Terry Hennessey	39 caps	Mark Crossley	8 caps
Ronnie Rees	39 caps	Darren Ward	5 caps
Chris Gunter	25 caps		

FOREST LEGEND – WALLY ARDRON

Centre-forward Walter 'Wally' Ardron was born in Swinton-on-Dearne on 19 September 1918 and joined Forest in July 1949 for a fee of around £10,000. He netted 124 times for the Reds in 191 appearances, until his retirement in 1955. This great header of the ball bagged 5 league hat-tricks plus 1 in the FA Cup. Sadly, Wally died in 1978.

YOU'LL NEVER BEAT DES WALKER

This was Forest fans' regular chant to away fans – and boy was this lad quick. Desmond Sinclair Walker was one of the greatest defenders ever to wear the red of Nottingham Forest. He joined as an apprentice in June 1982, turned professional in December 1983, and went on to make 387 appearances for the club, plus 8 as substitute, scoring 1 goal. Born in Hackney, London, on 26 November 1965, Des won two League Cup winner's medals with Forest in 1989 and 1990, also playing for Forest in the losing 1992 final. Des also had the misfortune of scoring an own-goal in Forest's 2–1 1991

FA Cup final defeat to Tottenham Hotspur. He was also a member of Forest's 1989 Simod Cup- and 1992 Zenith Data Systems Cup-winning teams. On the international stage Des Walker won 59 full international caps for England, to add to his 7 under-21 caps. He left Forest to join Sampdoria in Italy for a reported fee of £1.5 million in August 1992, returning to England in July 1993 when he joined Sheffield Wednesday for £2.7 million. Des also played a season at Burton Albion in 2001/02, before rejoining Forest in July 2002. After a disastrous 2001/02 when he was sidelined through injury for almost the whole season, Des returned to full fitness and was in superb form in 2002/03 when his vast experience shone through as Forest battled into the play-offs.

Des Walker was widely regarded as a brilliant and reliable centre-back, skilful and unflappable under pressure. Consistent, an outstanding tackler, a brilliant reader of the game with a unique positional sense – to name just a few of the complimentary plaudits heaped upon this excellent professional. However, for many, his greatest attribute was his uncanny speed over the ground that so often saw him win the ball from his opponents. Des Walker marshalled his defence like a great general. He is, and is sure to remain, a firm fans' favourite.

FOREST LEGEND – PETER WITHE

Born in Liverpool on 30 August 1951, Peter Withe made a few appearances for Southport, Preston North End and Barrow, before trying his luck in South Africa with Port Elizabeth & Arcadia Shepherds, where he was spotted and recommended to Wolves. He joined Wolves on loan in September 1973, before signing for £13,500 one month later. For the Molineux outfit he played only another 14 games, plus 3 as substitute, scoring 3 goals, before moving to Portland Timbers in the NASL. He joined Birmingham City for £50,000 (his registration was still owned by Wolves) in August 1975 and that's where Brian Clough, not a bad judge of centre-forwards, saw him and decided he would do a good job for Forest. He was brought to the City Ground in September 1976 for a fee of £42,000. Clough sold Withe to Newcastle for £200,000 in September 1978, after only 75 league appearances for the Reds, including 1 as substitute, and 28 league goals. Was the 'Old Master' too quick to cash in on his centre-forward? Withe stayed in the North-East until being bought by Aston Villa in May 1980 for a transfer fee of £500,000, where he won his second Championship-winner's medal in 1980/81, scoring the winning goal for Villa in the European Champions Cup final in 1982. He made 233 appearances for Villa and scored a very creditable 92 goals. He was capped 11 times for England, scoring 1 goal, often teaming-up with his former Forest strike-partner Tony Woodcock. His first cap was against Brazil in 1981, his last in the 8–0 thrashing of Turkey in the World Cup qualifying match in Istanbul, in an England team that included a few familiar Forest faces, old and current: Shilton, Anderson, Francis and Woodcock. In July 1985 he moved on a free transfer to Sheffield United, and then went on loan to Birmingham City between September and November 1987. Next he went to Huddersfield Town as player-coach in July 1988, and subsequently in 1991 to Aston Villa as assistant manager/coach to Josef Venglos. From there Peter tried management with Wimbledon from October 1991 to January 1992. In a long career, Peter Withe played in excess of 600 games and scored more than 200 goals.

FOREST LEGEND – TONY WOODCOCK

Tony was born in Nottingham on 6 December 1955, signing apprentice forms for Forest in January 1974 and making his first-team debut on 24 April 1974 in the 3–1 defeat by Aston Villa at Villa Park – the penultimate game of the season.

He also played in the final game, a 2–0 win away at Portsmouth. In the following season, 1974/75, he made 5 appearances, plus 4 as substitute, but didn't score in any of these games. He was then loaned to Doncaster Rovers and Lincoln City to hone his goalscoring technique and his confidence. He returned to the Forest side on 6 November 1976, getting his first senior goal one week later in the 1–0 win at Orient, going on to score 11 League goals in 30 appearances in that promotion-winning season. In all he made 125 league appearances for Forest, plus 4 as substitute, scoring 36 league goals. The PFA's Young Player of the Year in 1978, Woodcock won 42 caps for England, scoring 16 goals. A bit surprisingly, Clough sold him to German Bundesliga side Cologne in November 1979, the club that Forest had beaten 4–3 on aggregate in the semi-finals of the European Cup in April 1979. Tony Woodcock later joined Arsenal in July 1982.

THE LAST WORD GOES TO CLOUGHIE ...

'They say Rome wasn't built in a day, but I wasn't on that particular job.'

Cloughie's view on his own ability

'When I go, God's going to have to give up his favourite chair.'

Cloughie's view on dying

'I want no epitaphs of profound history and all that type of thing. I contributed. I would hope they would say that, and I would hope somebody liked me.'

Clough on being remembered

'The River Trent is lovely. I know because I have walked on it for 18 years.'

Cloughie on the River Trent

ACKNOWLEDGEMENTS

I would like to say a big thank you to the following people for the assistance they have given to me during the production of this book. In particular to Michelle Tilling, Richard Leatherdale and everyone at The History Press, without whom this book may never have been finished. Also, my thanks to Ken Sharpe, ex-Nottingham Forest youth player and Tom Sharpe, ex-Nottingham Forest squad member and youth player.

A huge extra special thank you to the directors, management, players and staff at Nottingham Forest, and to everyone who has helped me with proof-reading, or has provided information about Nottingham Forest. Finally, thanks to my long-suffering wife Kate and my sons John and Peter.

Every effort has been made to ensure the accuracy of the facts included in this book, however the author and publisher apologise should any inaccuracies have inadvertently crept in.